Praise for IMAGINE: Livin

"Throughout history, those who have sought radical change have always had to first discredit the ideas used to prop up ruling elites and construct alternative ideas for society. The articulation of a viable socialism as an alternative to corporate tyranny is, for me, paramount. Once ideas shift for a large portion of a population, once the vision of a new society grips the popular imagination, the old regime is finished. That is why *Imagine: Living in a Socialist USA* is an important contribution in promoting revolutionary ferment and consciousness."

—Chris Hedges, author of *Death of the Liberal Class*

"The best, most insightful, and most lively work on socialism to appear in a long time. Its unique approach gives readers a chance to renew the future-vision that once, long ago, put Edward Bellamy's *Looking Backward* onto the all-time bestsellers' list and even converted Eugene Debs. This book is bound to have a big impact on the way we view our country."

—Paul Buhle, author of *Marxism in the United States*

"The death of capitalism, sooner rather than later, is a certainty. Yet scenarios for transition to socialism, the only system that can save humanity from the accumulated contradictions of its past, are both scarce and often so generalized as to be useless to those locked in today's desperate struggles. How does the great human constellation make the epochal break, from our particular spaces in the here and now? In answering this question, socialists must apply universal principles to a whole world of particularities, starting with the movements in which they are directly engaged. *Imagine: Living in a Socialist USA* has gathered under one cover some of the most gifted thinkers and activists of the American Left, men and women for whom socialism is the compass that points to radical transformation—a world put on new footing, snatched back from the precipice."

—Glen Ford, executive editor, *Black Agenda Report*

IMAGINE
LIVING IN A
SOCIALIST USA

Edited by Frances Goldin,
Debby Smith, and
Michael Steven Smith

HARPER PERENNIAL

NEW YORK • LONDON • TORONTO • SYDNEY • NEW DELHI • AUCKLAND

HarperCollins books may be purchased for educational, business, or sales promotional use. For information please e-mail the Special Markets Department at SPsales@harpercollins.com.

FIRST EDITION

Designed by Michael Correy

Printed on acid-free paper

Library of Congress Cataloging-in-Publication Data

Goldin, Frances.

  Imagine : living in a socialist USA / Frances Goldin. — First edition.

    pages cm.

  ISBN 978-0-06-230557-2 (pbk.) — ISBN 978-0-06-230558-9 (e-book)
1. Socialism—United States. 2. Political participation—United States. 3.
United States—Politics and government—21st century. I. Title.

  HX89.G58 2014

  335.00973—dc23

                                 2013026749

ISBN 978-0-06-230557-2   (pbk.)

14 15 16 17 18   OV/RRD   10 9 8 7 6 5 4 3 2 1

We go forward to preserve the air and land and water and sky and all the beasts that crawl and fly. We go forward to safeguard the right to speak and write, to join, to learn, to rest, safe at home, to be secure, fed, healthy, sheltered, loved and loving, to be at peace with our identity.

—*Lynne Stewart*

Imagine no possessions
I wonder if you can
No need for greed or hunger
A brotherhood of man
Imagine all the people
Sharing all the world . . .

You may say I'm a dreamer
But I'm not the only one
I hope someday you'll join us
And the world will live as one

—*John Lennon, "Imagine"*

CONTENTS

Section 3:
Getting There: How to
Make a Socialist America 197

PREFACE

I have lived a very long and fruitful life, and I have very few regrets about the path I have walked. There are but two more things I am determined to achieve before I join my ancestors.

One is to join with others to free Mumia Abu-Jamal from the bars that constrain him. This innocent man has never allowed anyone or anything to silence his condemnation of our government's wrongdoings or of the powers that keep him imprisoned. Ever outspoken, his books speak truth to power in a way that most mortals have forsaken. This extraordinary, radical intellectual must be free to teach new generations how to build a better world.

The other is to create this book, which describes what socialism would look like in the United States of America. Imagine that!

The ignorance about what socialism really is and how it could be realized here in our own country is appalling. The mainstream media and the powers that be have made the word "socialism" frightening, foreign, unpatriotic, and menacing. It threatens their ill-gotten gains, so the idea of workers sharing in the wealth that their sweat and toil has generated has to be labeled "un-American." "Sharing the wealth" scares the "1 percent" and provokes them to quash, arrest, and jail those—like the members of the Occupy movement—who dare to challenge their power.

But a better world is possible, and if we are to win any measure of justice in our country, we must all take responsibility for working toward it. As the drums beat for more wars, there is an alternative: give the power back to the working people—or risk turning into a barbaric, fascist state.

Nowhere in the world would socialism be more feasible than in our United States. Imagine full employment, universal health care, and free advanced education for all. Imagine guaranteeing women full equality—including equal pay for equal work. Imagine an end to discrimination against gays, lesbians, bisexuals, and transgender men and women. Imagine the end of all wars of aggression and the demise of the military-industrial complex. Imagine doing away with the prison-industrial complex, the death penalty, racial profiling, and the mass incarceration of black youth. Imagine putting music and art back into refurbished schools, raising wages for *all* workers, building millions of affordable apartments in cities and providing affordable homes to all in need.

It's not a dream. It can be done if the people struggle to replace rapacious capitalism with life-enhancing socialism.

—*Frances Goldin*

Introduction

IMAGINE: Living in a Socialist USA

This book was Frances Goldin's idea. She said to us, "I'm eighty-eight years old. I want to do two things before I die: get Mumia Abu-Jamal out of prison and edit a book about what America might be like if it were socialist."

It is one thing to criticize what *is*—that's easy. But to imagine what *might be* is not. Even Karl Marx didn't attempt it. But things have changed since the mid-nineteenth century—for better and for worse.

We certainly know where things are heading. Rosa Luxemburg proposed two stark choices just after the imperialist slaughter that was World War I: socialism or barbarism. Given the catastrophe of climate change, the ongoing economic upheaval, and the risk of nuclear annihilation, it'll be barbarism—if we're lucky.

We are running out of time. There must be a future for a radical mass movement, or there will be no future at all. This is a book of imagination, not utopian fantasy. What it envisions— what it hopes for—is eminently possible. And without hope, as our friend Ramsey Clark says, what's the use of doing anything? Indeed, it is ultimately hope that the authors write about. "At the risk of sounding ridiculous," as Che Guevara once said, they imagine a world of love and solidarity.

The book is divided into three parts. The first is an indictment of American capitalism. The second part is intended to inspire hope: it imagines what life in America would be like if capitalism were overthrown. It covers multiple aspects of the new world: art, health care, housing, food, emotional life, sexuality, racism, criminal justice, poverty, immigration, religion, drugs, education, science and technology, women, ecology, and the democratic organization of a publicly owned economy. The third part discusses how to get from where we are to where we want to be.

This isn't utopian, either. It's been done before—or more precisely, it's been attempted. But the Russians discovered that you can't implement socialism in a poor, underdeveloped country ravaged by World War I, during which it was invaded by a number of European countries (plus a small US force) in an attempt to restore capitalist property relations. It was subsequently embargoed by those same countries. By 1991, the Soviets had been worn down.

It was attempted in China, a desperately poor country ravaged by years of Western imperial plunder, by the Japanese during World War II, and then, after their 1949 revolution, forsaken by the Soviet Union and embargoed by the West.

It was attempted in Vietnam after its eight-year war of independence from France. But then the United States invaded, dropping more than three times the tonnage of bombs that it dropped on Germany and Japan in World War II, defoliating the countryside with cancer-causing chemicals, and killing some three million Vietnamese.

It was attempted in Cuba. Just ninety miles off the coast of Florida, its development has been stunted by a hostile US embargo in spite of which it has made great advances in health care, putting the US health-care system to shame.

So why would it be different in the United States? Because the United States is the richest country the world has ever seen. Conditions are ripe—indeed overripe—for these resources to be utilized for the good of all, not for the profit of a few, for the 1 percent. But how do we get to where we want to be? The question will be answered by the masses of people—and their dedicated and experienced leaders—who can put the lessons of past struggles to use in both their organizing and their goals.

There is plenty of wisdom in this book: in its authors' understanding of capitalism and its depredations; in their proposals for how to replace it, and with what—in their vision of what might be. Read it and make the most of it.

Debby Smith
Michael Steven Smith
New York, New York
October 2012

Section 1

WHAT'S WRONG WITH CAPITALISM?

Chapter 1

Capitalism: The Real Enemy

Paul Street

I threw families onto the street in Iraq only to come home and find families thrown onto the street in this country in this tragic and unnecessary foreclosure crisis. We need to wake up and realize that our real enemies are not in some distant land, and not people whose names we don't know and cultures we don't understand. The enemy is people we know very well and people we can identify. The enemy is a system that wages war when it's profitable. The enemy is the CEOs who lay us off from our jobs when it's profitable. It's the insurance companies who deny us health care when it's profitable. It's the banks who take away our homes when it's profitable. Our enemies are not 5,000 miles away: they are right here at home.

—Mike Prysner, testimony to the Iraq Veterans Against the War "Winter Soldier" Hearings, March 13, 2008

Mike Borosky's Story

Where to begin in evoking the horrors of capitalism in the contemporary United States? We could start with the experience of Mike Borosky, a former factory worker from Pennsylvania. In

January 2011, while the media focused on the democratic up-heavals in Tunisia and Egypt, Borosky learned that the Coleman pop-up camper trailer factory in the town of Somerset, where he had been employed for more than thirty years, was shutting its doors. He got the news just as his wife was being wheeled into an operating room for spinal surgery.

"I was numb," Borosky, then fifty-three, remembers. "My wife had just gone in for surgery, and I didn't even have a job. I wasn't even thinking that I didn't have health insurance."

It probably didn't take long for that second terrible thought to register. The United States is the only country among modern industrialized "democracies" that doesn't provide universal health care for its people. With its archaic system of employment-based health insurance, it is a nation in which workers fear not merely the loss of their jobs but consequently losing health insurance coverage for themselves and their families as well.

Soon Borosky learned that FTCA Inc., which had taken over the Coleman plant years before, had failed to pay the health insurance premiums for its workers. That left him stuck with more than $63,000 in medical bills. FTCA was owned by Blackstreet Capital, a private-equity firm that managed hundreds of millions of dollars in investment capital. Blackstreet claimed there were no funds left to pay the Coleman plant's 150 employees any of the benefits owed them under their union contract. FTCA abruptly closed the factory without issuing the 60-day notice required under federal law. It cancelled workers' health insurance and refused to pay severance and accrued vacation time or to make good on the contributions it owed to their 401(k) retirement accounts.

Borosky's story was told in the winter 2012 issue of the United Steelworkers' (AFL-CIO) magazine. That issue also reported that Whirlpool, the world's leading appliance manufacturing corporation, would soon close its large refrigerator plant in Fort Smith, Arkansas, and send much of its production to Ramos Arizpe, Mexico. Whirlpool blamed sluggish demand for appliances—the same reason it gave in 2010 for closing a refrigerator factory in Evansville, Indiana, and transferring that plant's work to Mexico. That move cost the United States a thousand jobs, a standard chapter in the familiar story of capitalists' longstanding "globalization" campaign. The company had nothing to say about its thirst to boost profits by exploiting cheap labor and weaker environmental regulations abroad.

"Profits Booming, Why Not Jobs?"

A *New York Times* article published around the same time that Mike Borosky got knocked numb by Blackstreet Capital was titled "Profits Are Booming, Why Not Jobs?" *Times* business correspondent Michael Powell reported that corporate "earnings" had exploded "even as fifteen million Americans remain mired in unemployment, a number without precedent since the Great Depression" and while the citizenry experienced "record levels of foreclosures and indebtedness." At the current sluggish level of job growth, Powell noted, the US economy would require seven and a half years just to replace the jobs lost at the beginning of the Great Recession of 2008–2009. Another five million jobs would be needed just for employment to keep up with population growth.

Meanwhile, American businesses reported that profits in the third quarter of 2010 had risen at an annual rate of $1.66 trillion, "the steepest annual surge since officials began tracking such matters 60 years ago. It was the seventh consecutive quarter in which corporate profits climbed," Powell noted.

Powell found numerous reasons for the profits-jobs disconnect. US-based corporations now made a remarkable portion of their profits overseas. Thanks to lax American tax laws, "these companies return fewer of those profits to American shores than in the past."

Some big American firms were showing higher profits simply because their competition had collapsed. After the financial crash of 2008, for example, Wall Street giants Goldman Sachs and JPMorgan Chase no longer had to compete with Bear Stearns, Lehman Brothers, and Merrill Lynch. Many jobs disappeared with the departure of the defeated firms.

In the wake of the crash, many companies sat on capital and stored up liquidity like never before. Firms who no longer believed they could borrow quickly decided to keep a lot more cash on hand as a precaution. The falling interest rates produced by the recession gave corporations an incentive to simply "exploit the spread" between the low cost of borrowing and the higher rates of return on federal Treasury bonds they purchased with cheap loans. This let them make money without selling much or hiring new workers.

Meanwhile, a large reserve army of unemployed workers was a profits boon to corporate America. Desmond Lachman, a former managing director at Salomon Smith Barney and now a "scholar" at the American Enterprise Institute, an influential right-wing think tank, spoke about this candidly. "Corporations," Lachman told Powell, "are taking huge advantage of the slack in the labor market—they are in a very strong position and workers are in a very weak position. They are using that bargaining power to cut benefits and wages, and to shorten hours"—and thereby to increase profits.

"A Harsh Environment Is a Good Thing"

"American" capital was also continuing to shift jobs to lower-wage countries. In the era of global capitalism, US capital has gravitated to places like Foxconn's Longhua factory campus in

Shenzhen, China, where wages are low enough for the company to "make products like the [Apple] iPhone at seemingly impossible prices," as *Bloomberg Businessweek* wrote.

The entrance to the Longhua campus, the magazine said, "looks like a border crossing, with seven tollbooth-like lanes and uniformed guards." It has 300,000 workers, who also manufacture Sony PlayStations and Dell computers.

Foxconn employs more than 920,000 workers across 20 mainland Chinese factories. It manufactures products for leading "American" multinational corporations, including IBM, Cisco, Microsoft, and Hewlett-Packard. The workers, mostly 18-to-25-year-olds from rural areas, live in dormitories and are paid a mere $176 per month. The conditions are so alienating that 11 workers committed suicide in early 2010, most of them by leaping from the high-rise dormitories. The company subsequently strung more than 30 million square feet of yellow nets around its buildings and set up a 24-hour counseling center with 100 workers on staff.

The "drab and utilitarian" production complex, as *Businessweek* described it, includes "huge LED screens that flash public-service announcements and cartoons" and a bookstore that sells the Chinese-language translation of the *Harvard Business Review*. The bookstore prominently displays biographies of Foxconn CEO Terry Gou, the "Henry Ford of China" and the richest man in Taiwan; *Forbes* estimates his personal fortune at $5.9 billion. One of the Gou biographies collects his many pithy aphorisms, including the following Dickensian maxims: "Work itself is a type of joy," "Hungry people have especially clear minds," and "A harsh environment is a good thing."

The arduous nature of working-class life in Shenzhen and similar manufacturing zones around the world—Bangladesh, the Philippines, the *maquiladoras* along the US-Mexican border—is a leading reason why US workers now make only a small portion of many of the consumer goods sold in the United States. A harsh environment for developing-country workers is a good (i.e., profitable) thing for globally mobile "American" capital.

"Ready to Lead"

The American "homeland" has also become a much harsher environment for its working-class citizens. Mike Borosky's ordeal is one of millions unfolding at the hands of capital here. Since the monumental financial collapse in the fall of 2008 that shook the world and plunged the United States into an epic recession, the signs of destitution have intensified:

- The 2010 Census revealed that a record-setting one in fifteen Americans now live in "deep poverty," on an income of less than $11,157 for a family of four—less than half the amount the federal government defines as "poverty."
- By 2010, the total number of Americans living in official poverty reached a historic high of 46.2 million. Over 15 percent of the nation's population (more than one in seven Americans) lived below the federal poverty line, on incomes of less than $11,139 for a single person or $22,314 for a family of four, a standard that many consider grossly inadequate.
- By 2011, one in six Americans (fifty million, a population twice the size of Texas) had no health insurance, and 14.5 percent of American households were defined as "food insecure"—having difficulties putting enough food on the table.
- A Census report commissioned by the *New York Times* in the fall of 2011 showed that one in three Americans lived either in official poverty or in "near poverty," at less than 150 percent of the poverty level.
  As usual, the crisis fell hardest on people of color:

- Four of every ten black people of working age were unemployed at some point during 2008 and 2009.
- In thirty-five of America's biggest cities, during the first half of 2010, the official joblessness rate among black people ranged from 30 to 35 percent—a measure equal to the worst days of the Great Depression.
- The real combined unemployment rate for black and Latino workers (including workers who were involuntarily underemployed) in 2010 was 25 percent.
- The black poverty rate rose to 26 percent, double that of white poverty.
- The difference between the median wealth of white and black households rose to nearly 15 to 1. The median black household's net worth was only 7 percent of the median white household's.
- By 2010, more than half the homes bought by black Americans in 2006 had been foreclosed on.
- In 2010, an astonishing half of all US children and 90 percent of black US children had depended on food stamps at some point during their lives.

A De Facto Dictatorship in the Heartland of "The Beacon to the World of the Way Life Should Be"

The Whirlpool Corporation's sprawling and plush global headquarters is located on the edge of Benton Harbor, Michigan. Its predominantly white managers and staff steer clear of the city proper, whose 11,000 people are 89 percent black. Site of a riot sparked by police brutality in the summer of 2003 (the National Guard was called in), Benton Harbor has a poverty rate of more than 50 percent, a child poverty rate above 60 percent, a deep poverty rate of 26 percent, and a per capita income of around $10,000.

It is plagued by the standard ills that accompany poverty in the militantly business-ruled nation that Senator Kay Bailey Hutchinson (R-Texas) once called "the beacon to the world of the way life should be": mass unemployment, failing and under-funded schools, crime, drugs, broken government, and endemic despair. Over the last thirty-five years, the once-thriving manufacturing town has been stripped of industrial jobs (Whirlpool and other local manufacturers left for cheaper labor elsewhere); of retail stores (Sears and J.C. Penney left town years ago); of environmental health (the departing manufacturers left behind hundreds of acres of polluted fields and wetlands, including a Superfund site contaminated by radioactive paint); of a favorite local beach (recently appropriated by Whirlpool and upscale developers to create a fancy lakeside golf resort); and now even of its last remnants of formal democracy.

In April 2011, Benton Harbor's local government was handed over to an "emergency fiscal manager"—a de facto dictator appointed to run the city under a chilling law passed by Michigan's militantly pro-corporate governor and state legislature. Governor Rick Snyder issued an order removing all powers from the local city council. As the Reverend Jesse Jackson said soon afterward, "No money can be spent, no taxes raised or lowered, no bonds issued, no regulations changed without his approval."

This can accurately be described as "fiscal martial law." In the name of balancing the city's budget, the new czar can sell public assets, revoke labor contracts, dismiss pension boards, and take over pension funds.

Jamie Dimon's "Earnings": $57,000 a Day

While lower- and working-class people suffer—particularly people of color—a tiny minority is accruing obscene fortunes and sits atop huge piles of capital. There are more than 3.1

million millionaires in the United States: the proverbial "1 percent."

Above them are the not quite 57,000 people (0.05 percent of the US population) who have been identified by the global wealth-intelligence firm Wealth X as "ultra-high net worth" individuals. The firm defines these outrageously rich people as anyone with at least $30 million in wealth, "including shares in companies, real estate, cash, art collections, private planes, and other investable assets."

At the very top, "the beacon to the world of the way life should be" has over 400 billionaires. At the pinnacle, according to *Forbes* magazine's list in early 2012, are three men: Bill Gates (net worth $61 billion), Warren Buffett ($44 billion), and Lawrence Ellison ($36 billion). Their combined wealth exceeded the total recession-induced budget shortfalls of every US state government in 2011.

The ultra-rich club includes J.P. Morgan CEO Jamie Dimon, whose net worth is $200 million. According to the *Wall Street Journal* in April 2011:

> *$57,031. That's about what the average US archaeologist made last year. It's also what Jamie Dimon made every day of last year—$20.8 million total, according to the firm's proxy filing this week. Anyone who has doubts about the resiliency of Wall Street banks and brokerages should ponder that figure for a while. The J.P. Morgan board also spent about $421,500 to sell Dimon's Chicago home. And they brought back the big cash bonus, doling out $30.2 million in greenbacks to Dimon and his top six lieutenants.*

Dimon and his fellow ultra-rich are touchstones of what is by far the industrialized world's most unequal society. By the eve of the crash, in 2007, the richest 1 percent of Americans owned more than a third of the nation's wealth and more than half of its financial wealth. The top tenth owned two-thirds, and the top fifth owned 85 percent, leaving the bottom four-fifths to fight it out for just one-sixth of the nation's wealth. The 120 million people in the bottom two-fifths owned 0.3 percent—essentially nothing.

Six members of the Walton family, the five children and one daughter-in-law of Walmart founders Sam and James "Bud" Walton, had a total net worth of $69.7 billion in 2011, labor economist Sylvia Allegretto estimates. This was equal to the total wealth of the entire bottom 30 percent, she found, citing the triennial Survey of Consumer Finances. It was a remarkable finding, given that Walmart pays wages so low that nearly a third of its workforce receives some kind of public assistance. The company was then cutting health-care coverage for part-time workers and raising premiums for many full-time staff. And Walmart is perhaps more responsible than any other company for transferring American manufacturing to China, as it is constantly demanding lower prices from its suppliers.

Such were the terrible and economically unsustainable consequences of what former United Auto Workers president Douglas Fraser in 1978 called the "one-sided class war" that corporate and financial America has waged on working-class incomes since the 1970s. Between 1983 and 2001, the top 1 percent of Americans gobbled up 28 percent of the rise in American income, 33 percent of the gain in national wealth, and 52 percent of the growth in financial net worth. In 2007, the one percent "earned" 23 percent of the nation's income, more than twice the share they had in 1986. Between the 1970s and the first decade of the twenty-first century, median pay for executives at the nation's largest companies more than quadrupled (after adjusting for inflation). In the same period, pay for a typical non-supervisory worker dropped more than 10 percent.

The nation's wealth inequality deepened after the crash, thanks to the devastation wreaked on housing values. Housing is the largest part of middle- and working-class families' net worth; in 2007, the bottom 60 percent of Americans had 65 percent of their net worth tied up in their homes. In contrast, the top 1 percent held just 10 percent of their wealth in personal real estate. The housing crisis has therefore inflated the share of total wealth held by the super-rich and deflated the share held by the bottom 60 percent.

A Blunt Lesson About Power

Amid the rising misery of the 2008 crash, the "people's government" in Washington, DC, scuttled about, scheming to bail out and protect the corporate and financial institutions that had crashed the economy. This was a completely bipartisan affair. The epic transfer of trillions of taxpayer dollars to Wall Street started under President George W. Bush and proceeded to record-setting levels under Barack Obama. It was not accompanied by any comparable aid for the millions of Americans who were running out of ammunition in the war on destitution. It was not matched by any remotely adequate government investment in urgently needed public works and jobs programs, housing assistance, or cash assistance for families.

The liberal commentator William Greider put it well in March 2009, when the Treasury Department announced that the Wall Street mega-firm AIG would be receiving an additional $30 billion in federal assistance on top of the $60 billion it had already gotten, even after news emerged that AIG had paid out $165 million in bonuses to its top managers. "People everywhere [have] learned a blunt lesson about power, who has it and who doesn't," Greider wrote in the *Washington Post*: "They [have] watched Washington run to rescue the very financial interests that caused the catastrophe. They [have] learned that government has plenty of money to spend when the right people want it."

Indeed, the Obama administration has provided a tutorial on who really rules America. The "change" and "hope" presidency brilliantly demonstrated the reach of what Edward S. Herman and David Peterson call "the unelected dictatorship of money," which vetoes any official who might seek "to change the foreign or domestic priorities of the imperial US regime."

Along with continuing the monumental bailout of the ultra-rich financial overlords, the Obama administration refused to nationalize or even significantly regulate the parasitic financial institutions that had paralyzed the economy. It passed a health-insurance bill that only the big insurance and drug companies could love. It cut a bailout deal with the automobile industry that rewarded capital flight and raided union pension funds. It undermined desperately needed global efforts to reduce carbon emissions at conferences in Copenhagen in 2009 and Durban in 2011. It refused to develop serious public-works programs (green or otherwise). It green-lighted offshore drilling and other en-vironmentally disastrous practices. It extended Bush's tax cuts for the rich. It froze federal wages and salaries. It made a debt-ceiling deal in 2011 that would slash social programs instead of raising taxes on the rich. It disregarded its promises to labor and repeatedly betrayed the constituencies in its progressive base.

Meanwhile, it kept the promises it made to its Wall Street and corporate sponsors, who had set new campaign finance rec-ords in backing Obama in 2008.

In the summer of 2011, at the height of the "debt-ceiling cri-sis" manufactured by the elite, one issue of the *New York Times* suggested the limits of "change." A front-page story reported on the House Republicans' false claim that increasing taxes on the rich would undermine corporate investment in the jobs that American workers desperately needed. Another was titled "Even

Marked Up, Luxury Goods Fly Off Shelves." While overall consumer spending continued to languish amid a "human recession" that lingered despite the "statistical recovery" announced earlier that year, the wealthy few were resuming their ways of conspicuous luxury consumption:

> *Nordstrom has a waiting list for a Chanel sequined tweed coat with a $9,010 price tag. Neiman Marcus has sold out in almost every size of Christian Louboutin "Bianca" platform pumps, at $775 a pair. Mercedes-Benz said it sold more cars last month in the United States than it had in any July in five years. . . .*
>
> *Even with the economy in a funk and many Americans pulling back on spending, the rich are again buying designer clothing, luxury cars and about anything that catches their fancy. Luxury goods stores, which fared much worse than other retailers in the recession, are more than recovering—they are zooming. Many high-end businesses are even able to mark up, rather than discount, items to attract customers who equate quality with price. . . .*
>
> *The luxury category has posted 10 consecutive months of sales increases compared with the year earlier,* even as overall consumer spending on categories like furniture and electronics has been tepid *[emphasis added].*

Dewey's Dark Cloud

The terrible signs of savage inequality and plutocracy have emerged despite the sentiments of the majority of Americans. Poll after poll shows that most Americans believe that job creation should be a bigger government priority than deficit reduction, that social protections should be expanded and not contracted, that the rich don't pay enough in taxes, that economic inequality and poverty are the nation's leading moral issues, that big business and the wealthy exercise too much influence over elections and policy, that government dollars should be significantly transferred from military to social programs, that Social Security and Medicare benefits should be protected and expanded, and that public-sector workers deserve collective-bargaining rights. But in 2011, when numerous Republican-controlled state governments tried to obliterate public workers' rights, there was no meaningful opposition from the Obama White House.

None of this majority progressive opinion ever seems to matter very much in the United States. Here, as the philosopher John Dewey wrote nearly a century ago, "politics is the shadow cast on society by big business."

The nation's gaping "democratic deficit" is a much greater problem than its much-bemoaned fiscal deficit. As Noam Chomsky noted in 2011, "Since the 1970s, [Dewey's] shadow has become a dark cloud enveloping society and the political system. Corporate power, by now largely financial capital, has reached the point that both political organizations, which now barely resemble traditional parties, are far to the right of the population on the major issues under debate."

"We the people" are *not* sovereign in the failed state that is the twenty-first-century United States. Capital rules, over and against the will of the citizenry and the common good.

Capitalism vs. Democracy

Those who find this difficult to believe because they have been taught to conflate capitalism with popular governance (as two sides of the same coin—"the single sustainable model for national success") should look at *Webster's New Twentieth-Century Dictionary* (unabridged and second edition, 1979). There,

cap'i-tal-ism, n. is defined as "the economic system in which all or most of the means of production and distribution as land, factories, railroads, etc., are privately owned and operated for profit, originally under fully competitive conditions; it has been generally characterized by a tendency toward concentration of wealth, and, in its later phases, by the growth of great corporations, increased government control, etc."

This definition does not mention any of the things routinely identified with capitalism in the dominant US political and intellectual discourse—democracy, freedom, trade, job creation, growth, and/or a "free market" that is characterized by widespread competition and/or little or no government interference. Capitalism is about profit for the owners of capital—period. They attain this through any number of means. The most damaging include:

- seizing others' land and materials
- slavery (the leading source of capital accumulation in the United States before it was outlawed in 1863–65)
- firing workers or replacing them with technology
- undermining the value and power of labor by "de-skilling" workers by reducing the amount of knowledge and experience they need to do their jobs
- outsourcing work to sections of the world economy with the lowest wages and the worst working conditions
- hiring and exploiting unprotected migrant workers
- slashing wages and benefits, or cheating workers out of them
- purely speculative investment
- forming monopolies and using them to raise prices
- dismantling competing firms, sectors, and industries
- deadly pollution and perversion of the natural environment
- appropriating public assets

- military contracting and war production
- working to shape political and intellectual culture and policy in their favor by funding political campaigns, hiring lobbyists, buying and controlling the media, manipulating public relations and propaganda, investing in the educational system, offering lucrative employment and other economic opportunities to policy makers and their families, holding key policy-making positions, and threatening to withdraw investment from places that don't submit to capital's rules while promising to invest in places that do.

When capitalism is understood for what it is really and only about—investor profit—there is nothing paradoxical about its failure to serve working people and the common good, much less the cause of democracy, in the United States or anywhere else. If corporate profits are high, the system is working for its architects and intended beneficiaries: capitalists. Its great corporations (now granted the legal protection of artificial personhood) are working precisely as they are supposed to under US law. This holds, as the Michigan Supreme Court ruled in Dodge v. Ford Motor Company in 1919, that "managers have a legal duty to put shareholders' interests above all others and no legal authority to serve any other interests."

One does not have to be a Marxist or other variety of radical to acknowledge the basic differences and fundamental conflicts between capitalism and democracy. "Democracy and capitalism have very different beliefs about the proper distribution of power," the liberal economist Lester Thurow noted in the mid-1990s. "One [democracy] believes in a completely equal distribution of political power, 'one man, one vote,' while the other [capitalism] believes that it is the duty of the economically fit to drive the unfit out of business and into extinction. . . . To put it in its starkest form, *capitalism is perfectly compatible with slavery. Democracy is not* [emphasis added]."

Chicago Tribune economics correspondent R. C. Longworth, also no radical, wrote in 1999 that the "struggle of democracy and capitalism" was at the heart of the debate over the global economy. In theory, he observed, "they are meant to go together, indeed to be inseparable. But democracy's priorities are equality before the law, the right of each citizen to govern the decisions that govern his or her life, the creation of a civilization based on fairness and equity. Capitalism's priorities are inequality of return, profit for the suppliers of capital . . . *the bottom line* [emphasis added]."

Capitalism vs. Survival

A beleaguered and destroyed natural environment is the ultimate "harsh environment" produced by the profit system. The enemy that radical veteran activist Mike Prysner spoke of is also a system that destroys a sustainable, life-supporting environment whenever it's profitable to do so The enemy is the CEOs who hire lobbyists and public relations firms to deny and discredit science's findings about global warming and related environmental disasters in the making.

According to research published in June 2012 by the science journal *Nature*, humanity is now facing imminent threat of extinction caused by its reckless exploitation of the natural environment. Our planet's biosphere is ever more rapidly approaching a tipping point: all of its ecosystems are undergoing an irreversible change that is rendering them inhospitable to human life.

"The data suggests that there will be a reduction in biodiversity and severe impacts on much of what we depend on to sustain our quality of life, including . . . fisheries, agriculture, forest products, and clean water. This could happen within just a few generations," wrote leading author Anthony Barnosky, a professor of integrative biology at the University of California-Berkeley.

"My colleagues who study climate-induced changes through the Earth's history are more than pretty worried," co-researcher Arne Mooers, a professor of biodiversity at Simon Fraser University in British Columbia, said in a statement. "In fact, some are terrified."

If this environmental catastrophe isn't averted, Noam Chomsky said in a widely read speech to Occupy Boston in 2011, then "in a generation or two, everything else we're talking about won't matter." Capitalism lies at the heart of this ecological crisis. It values private profit over the common good, a thing's selling price over the value of its social use. It insists on private management, to whom the short-term bottom line is more important than the long-term fate of the species. It has a deep investment in the carbon-addicted way of life and death. It depends on constant growth and accumulation. It is attached to a divided world of competing nations and corporate empires incapable of common action for the global good.

This is all incompatible with the profound changes required for humans and other life to survive the ecological crisis, rightly described by the radical philosopher John Sanbonmatsu as "the number one issue of our *or any time* [emphasis added]." Solving the crisis requires moving beyond the profit system.

The Real Issue

Months after its encampments were torn down—often with brute force and most often by Democratic city governments—the Occupy movement still deserves major credit for changing the nation's political discourse. By emphasizing economic inequality and the unmatched power of the wealthy few to destroy democracy, society, and the Earth's ecology, it called out the names and addresses of the true masters: corporate-financial capital and Wall Street.

If the Occupy movement and the movements that will carry on its spirit are to achieve real change on the scale required, they will have to confront the real enemy beneath and beyond "the 1 percent": the endlessly rapacious and ruthless socioeconomic system called capitalism.

The capitalist order is the taproot of economic collapse, social breakdown, imminent environmental collapse, and authoritarian state failure in both the United States and the world. John Dewey rightly prophesized that this would continue, that US politics would remain "the shadow cast on society by business" as long as power resides in "business for private profit through private control of banking, land, industry, reinforced by command of the press, press agents, and other means of publicity and propaganda."

We have been living with the dire consequences of that tyranny for far too long. The conclusion is unavoidable: reforms, while they'd improve people's lives, will not suffice. Fundamental social change leading us beyond the profit system is essential if we are going to bring meaningful democracy to the United States. As the great democratic socialist Martin Luther King Jr. noted in a posthumously published essay titled "A Testament of Hope," the real issue to be faced is "the radical reconstruction of society itself."

IMAGINING SOCIALISM

Chapter 2

The Future Will Be Ecosocialist, Because Without Ecosocialism, There Will Be No Future

Joel Kovel

Socialism was originally seen as victory in a struggle for justice. The proletarians, concluded the *Communist Manifesto* in 1848, "have nothing to lose but their chains. They have a world to win. *Working men of all countries unite!*"

All this remains true, although today we'd include women. Working women and men continue to suffer exploitation in the workplace and throughout a society ruled by capitalism's money-power. Increasing divisions of wealth and poverty, massive and chronic unemployment, the curse of indebtedness, the militarism of the state: all this and more afflict the people. Now, as in 1848, workers need a revolutionary socialist transformation. They need to unite, and to again quote the *Manifesto*, achieve "an association in which the free development of each is the condition of the free development of all."

But the world we have to win has profoundly changed from the world of 1848. It has to be saved from another terrible affliction. Human beings produce the things we use for our lives by changing nature, and the harm to nature wrought by human production has reached intolerable proportions. Climate change, massive species extinctions, and pollution on a scale never before encountered are all signs that humanity has destabilized nature to the point where Homo sapiens, a species that has triumphed over nature to build the mighty civilization that now rules over the Earth, may have also laid the foundation for its own extinction.

The Ecological Crisis and Capital Accumulation

Because our collective survival is at stake, humanity is facing its greatest challenge ever. Because it involves the relationships between ourselves and nature, and because the study of relationships between living creatures and their natural environment is named ecology, we can call it an ecological crisis.

Unhappily, despite a vast amount of scientific investigation into the individual disasters within this ecological crisis, there is very little awareness of its causes and real character. The dominant opinion sees the crisis as something between ourselves and "nature," an array of things outside ourselves. This overlooks that we are part of nature and its ecosystems.

We tend to think of environmental problems as a great set of discrete troubles, itemized like a huge shopping list and demanding individualized attention. They therefore get listed among other worthy causes, like jobs, health care, and the rights of sexual minorities. This version of environmentalism believes that regulations, legislation, and policy changes can solve ecological problems, under the watchful eye of bureaucracies such as the United Nations' massive carbon-regulation system or the US Environmental Protection Agency. It also seeks technical fixes or personal lifestyle changes, such as recycling or buying "green" products.

This idea of environmentalism has good intentions, but it focuses on the symptoms of the crisis and ignores the underlying disease. It fails to recognize that what is happening is the sign of a profound disorder. It does not ask what is wrong with a society that so ravages the Earth; it simply attempts to tidy up the mess in a piecemeal and fundamentally futile fashion—like treating cancer with aspirin for the pain and baths for the discomfort.

Of course, we need to meet every ecological threat vigorously. But we need to see the bigger picture as well. We are a part of nature, and our society reflects whether we are at home in it or estranged from it. Failure to understand this and to make the necessary changes in our relationship to nature puts the future of human life at risk, the lives of our children and grandchildren and all future generations, not to mention the innumerable other living things with whom we share our Planet Earth.

If the choices embedded in our society lead to ruin and death, then our obligation is to remake society from the ground up in the service of life. If this be read as a demand for revolution, so be it.

But a revolution of what kind?

Look at the society that rules the Earth and its guiding inner dynamic, the production of capital. However capitalism may be dressed up as a society of democracy, free markets, or progress, its first priority is profitability and, therefore, growth, the eternal expansion of the economic product. This requires converting everything possible into monetary value. The best word for that is "accumulation." The accumulation of capital is the supreme value of capitalists and all elements of capitalist society—control over resources, labor relations, fiscal and tax policy, culture and propaganda, the workings of academia, war, and imperialism—are shaped to satisfy its hunger.

Karl Marx saw the system as berserk and fundamentally uncontrollable. As he vividly wrote in *Capital*: "Accumulate! Accumulate! That is Moses and the prophets." In other words, capital is in the grip of a quasi-religious impulse that drives its system to convert the entire Earth—its oceans and atmosphere and everything under the sun—into commodities to be sold on the market, the profits converted to capital.

This leads to the obvious yet profound explanation of the ecological crisis and why it is life-threatening. The Earth we live on is finite, and its ecosystems have evolved to accommodate to that finitude. Therefore, a system built on endless growth is going to destroy the integrity of the ecosystems upon which life depends for food, energy, and other resources. It is also going to destroy the human ecosystems, or societies, that have emerged from nature to inhabit the planet. That this brutally clear truth is not widely accepted is partly the result of how hard it is to face up to so harsh a reality, but it is chiefly the result of the titanic effort waged by capitalist ideology to deny its responsibility for the ruin of Planet Earth.

Seen in this light, capitalism is truly pathological. It could be called a kind of metastasizing cancer, a disease that demands radical treatment—revolutionary change. Since socialism is (or should be) a movement to supersede capitalism, and because the present ecological crisis is driven by the accumulation of capital, we need to turn socialism to ecological ends as well as to providing justice to working people.

This means that socialism can no longer be the reformist social democracy that has betrayed its promise by seeking to perfect capitalism instead of going beyond it. Nor can it be a society in which nature is merely factored in. Our goal must be a society that serves the well-being of humanity and nature alike. Most critically, the new socialism must respect the notion of limits and consider production in ecological terms. The test of a viable and humanly worthwhile post-capitalist society is whether it can move from the generalized production of commodities to the production of flourishing, integral ecosystems. In doing so, socialism will become ecosocialism.

First Ecosocialist Lessons

We are nowhere near these goals. But that does not mean that we have no map of the route toward ecosocialism or of how to overcome the menace of climate change.

- Ecosocialism is still socialism. Its basic principle remains the core socialist principle of freely associated labor—the collective self-determination of producers released from the bondage of capitalist ownership of the means of production. It is built on the rational faith that women and men liberated from the tyranny of capitalism will use appropriate technology and organize their social relations and self-governance in a way that restores and preserves the integrity of nature. This is why it is essential to recognize our fundamental unity with nature and care for it as part of ourselves.

  The principle applies equally to caring for nature and providing a good life for humanity, although it redefines "the good life" as one freed from the compulsion to possess. We are indoctrinated by capitalist ideology from the cradle to the grave to consume more and more, to try to fill our inner emptiness with commodities. That mentality, and the dominion of commodities over life, inevitably lead to ecological crisis.

  As we break loose from the capitalist rat race, we will recognize ourselves as natural creatures and part of nature. This also applies to the so-called population problem, since freely associated human beings, and women in particular, will have no trouble at all in regulating their numbers.

  An ecosocialist society is animated by freely associated labor and guided by an ethic of ecological integrity. We free ourselves through collective struggle, which in ecosocialism is primarily about "commoning."

"The commons" denotes collectively owned sites of production. It also refers to the communalism of many "first peoples." Capitalism – rose by "enclosing" the commons, separating people from control over their productive activity and alienating them from nature and their own powers. The response of commoning can be as basic as making a community garden or day-care center. It extends all the way to building democratically organized intentional communities, and by extension, to a global society.

Ecosocialism has two aspects. One is resistance to capital and the capitalist state. The other is creating communities of production outside of hierarchical capitalist relations between the owners of the means of production and the "wage slaves" who feed the capital monster. Traditional labor organizing can include both of these aspects as long as it does not reproduce bureaucratic hierarchies and to the degree that it builds authentic "unions" and "solidarity"—terms that appear in both the language of ecology and the history of class struggle.

The wave of "occupations" that washed over the United States in the fall of 2011 were very much instances of commoning along ecosocialist lines. Many of their immediate demands may have seemed scattered and reformist, but the movement expressed our fundamental drive toward collective control over a commonly held space. The Occupy movements resisted established governmental and corporate ways, and created the potential for producing their own subsistence.

Seizing a kind of commons next to Wall Street simultaneously symbolized immediate demands for economic justice and prefigured liberated zones of ecosocialist production through freely associated labor. Prefiguration is a basic ecosocialist principle of building models for a future world beyond the death-dealing society of capital.

A sustainable and worthwhile future will be a network of commonal zones, beginning small but spreading and connecting across the artificial boundaries set up by class-based society and capital. Ecosocialism is transnational, global in scope, and, above all, visionary. Each local moment of commoning contains the germ of ecosocialist imagining. We see the coming-to-be of the new society in the scattered campgrounds of occupied zones within the capitalist order. Without vision, the people perish, as the saying goes. And with vision—and organizing to match—a new and better world can be won.

Ecosocialism Beyond Climate Change

Nothing represents the ecological horror induced by capitalism more than the specter of climate change. We stand on a crumbling precipice, our global ecosphere threatened by growing amounts of carbon dioxide pumped into the atmosphere by the hell-bent capitalist-industrial system. Much harm has already been done. And if we do not act successfully to reduce CO_2 emissions, far worse will come, as the consequences of a hotter atmosphere will interact to create a cascade of catastrophic climate events and associated nightmares such as mass starvation and pandemic diseases. This might doom us by the end of the century.

Two configurations are assembling to do battle over this future. One is directed by capital and the capitalist state. It is addicted to growth, rapacious for resources, and seeks to finagle its way out of the crisis through an utterly bankrupt system of commodifying nature and trading pollution credits. It seeks another path of accumulation while continuing to extract unlimited amounts of resources, the future be damned.

The second is ecosocialist. It brings together a coalition of ecosocialists, radical climate activists, and specialists in renewable energy from the global north and south. These groups increasingly work with indigenous folk whose lives are directly threatened by ever more violent methods of hydrocarbon extraction from places such as the Gulf of Mexico (deep offshore drilling), northern Alberta (tar-sands extraction), the Niger Delta and the Peruvian and Ecuadorian rainforests (rapacious oil drilling), West Virginia (mountaintop-removal mining for coal), and rural New York and Pennsylvania (hydro-fracking for natural gas). Its scope encompasses commoning, global resistance, and imagining a world beyond hydrocarbon-based industrialization, a world where production has been liberated from the compulsion to accumulate.

The best science tells us that this is the only path to survival. But the best science cannot be implemented within existing capitalism. It will take freely associated labor organized on a worldwide scale to effect these changes—to resist the fossil-fuel system, build an alternative, and then actualize that alternative: an economy that gets its energy from renewable sources such as solar power, wind, geothermal power, and tides. That is essential if we are to lower the level of atmospheric CO_2, which is now nearing an ultimately lethal 400 parts per million, to a sustainable 345 parts per million.

This may seem unthinkable, but is only so to minds chained to the ruinous and suicidal capitalist system. It's quite possible to envision how building renewable energy systems will cure the plague of worklessness that devastates contemporary society. Imagine the creative possibilities in an ecosocialist energy pathway. Then think and choose: should we keep the present system, or step forth into a renewed world?

Chapter 3

A Democratically Run Economy Can Replace the Oligarchy

Ron Reosti

It is increasingly apparent to most people that the United States is an oligarchy, not a democracy. An incredibly small number of very wealthy people (much smaller than 1 percent) have inordinate influence in the government, the media, academia, and most importantly, the economy.

These oligarchs are not, of course, elected. In fact, polls indicate that the majority in this country, the people who do the work that produces the oligarchs' immense fortunes, want a more egalitarian distribution of that wealth, a national health-care system, and secure retirement—all of which the economy can afford but which the oligarchs oppose.

These oligarchs exercise their control by virtue of their immense wealth, which enables them to finance both major political parties, own the major media outlets, and fund think tanks, university departments, and specialized political publications. They can reward those who promote capitalism and ostracize those who dare challenge their version of reality. Moreover, because they own and control the major corporations, most of the rest of us depend on them for our livelihoods. They determine what gets produced, where, when, by which means, and by whom. When they screw up, as in the latest crisis, we have to bail them out because if we do not, the entire economy would collapse, as it did in 1929!

We are constantly told that the American capitalist system is not just the best system—it is the *only* system that can provide a decent standard of living for the vast majority and preserve our democratic government. One reason the majority acquiesces to and even endorses this belief is that they are convinced that an egalitarian and democratic economy is a fantasy, that history proves that socialism equals dictatorship and poverty. But history is not destiny.

We are not a rural, uneducated peasant society. The idea that we cannot democratically design and control an economy that satisfies the needs and desires of the people without waste, inequities, wars, depressions, and environmental degradation is not just insulting—it is not true.

There are many economists, political scientists, and social scientists who have described how such an economy could work. They differ about how decisions would be made, but they are unanimous that the decision-making process must be democratic. This democracy is essential both to ensure against a dictatorship—whether it be a dictatorship of a bureaucracy, a political caste, or an oligarchy of capitalists—and also because democratic decision-making will ensure the most efficient use of resources (including labor) and the most efficient and equitable distribution of goods and services.

The best evidence that capitalists are not necessary is the success of hundreds of successful employee- and community-owned enterprises and co-ops that outperform their capitalist competitors.

There are over 11,000 businesses with employee stock-ownership plans (ESOPs) in the United States. Not all are totally employee-owned and -operated. But many are, and the evidence is that the more ownership and control the employees have, the more productive and successful is the enterprise. Gar Alperovitz, in his book *Beyond Capitalism,* catalogs some of the success stories, such as W. L. Gore, maker of Gore-Tex water-proof clothing. Studies by the National Center for Employee Ownership, several teams of economists, and the US General Accounting Office, he notes, "all confirm that combining work-er ownership and employee participation commonly produces greater productivity gains, in some cases over 50 percent."

Alperovitz also points out that there are over 48,000 co-ops now operating in the United States, including credit unions, ru-ral electric co-ops, retail co-ops, mutual insurance companies, and housing co-ops. In fact, he reports, 30 percent of US farm products are marketed through co-ops. These co-ops have over 120 million members, and many have been functioning for de-cades. Their members obviously prefer them to the capitalist alternatives.

Many communities have a long tradition of public owner-ship of banks, electric companies, water companies, hospitals, and, more recently, cable TV and Internet providers. Cleveland has had a publicly owned electric company since 1906. Publicly owned utilities on average charge their residential customers roughly 20 percent less than investor-owned utilities, and com-mercial customers pay 11 percent less. A 2000 study by Elliott Sclar of Columbia University suggested that the promised ben-efits of privatizing municipal electric utilities were illusory.

Some of these publicly owned enterprises date from the early twentieth century and continue to outperform private alterna-tives. The Bank of North Dakota was founded in 1919. Today it is still going strong, lending money to students, farmers, small businesses, and homeowners. In the two-year period from 2001 to 2003, the bank returned a profit of $75 to $80 million to the state. The Wisconsin State Life Insurance Fund, established in 1911, offers life insurance with premiums 10 to 40 percent lower than comparable private coverage and returned $3.7 to $3.9 million in dividends to policyholders in the 1990s. In Canada and the United Kingdom, national health plans provide better results at a significantly lower cost—without denying medical care to millions of citizens. (For more information, I recommend Erik Olin Wright's *Envisioning Real Utopias*.)

Even in large corporations, the workers handle the day-to-day operations—not the owners, stockholders, and financiers. This is important: despite the destructiveness of corporate power in our current society, some enterprises of that size will continue to exist in a socialist economy. Their economies of scale will be beneficial, provided they are run democratically.

Can such large, publicly owned corporations operate democratically, subject to a democratically determined central plan? If the criteria for an efficiently run large corporation are not about how much profit it makes for private investors but about how well it delivers the goods and services demanded by the community—with the minimum expenditure of resources and labor—there is no reason that it can't succeed. The Social Security Administration, the Veterans Administration hospitals, publicly owned utilities, and others all do so by this standard.

These institutions operate efficiently and are run by professional and dedicated employees. Millions of people depend on them for essential goods and services, and they are often responsible for and control billions of dollars. Despite the government's control of these programs, they have not established a dictatorship, and they are remarkably free of corruption. In fact, such government enterprises are examples of a democratic economy: they are ultimately subject to the will of the electorate. It should also be obvious that the more democratic, responsive, and truly representative the government, the more responsive will be the bureaucrats that it selects and hires to run these programs.

But is it enough that employee-owned and -controlled firms are more productive than comparable privately owned firms, and that publicly owned and operated businesses can compete with privately owned businesses? How does this guarantee that the *economy* would function efficiently if run democratically? How will investment priorities be decided? What will ensure that the necessary resources get to the firms that can best utilize them? How will a democratic socialist economy motivate workers to be efficient and creative?

Ironically, under capitalism, there is no guarantee that the economy will work efficiently—and certainly no guarantee of fairness or social welfare. Thousands of firms go bankrupt every year. The system experiences frequent recessions and, less frequently, disastrous depressions. These generate huge amounts of waste, the destruction or abandonment of productive equipment and buildings, and human suffering. Moreover, the so-called free market is unable to build infrastructure, provide education or health care, maintain social welfare, or ensure a livable environment. Government now provides most of these essential elements of an effective economy.

Some degree of central planning is both desirable and necessary. Even under capitalism, the Federal Reserve System decides monetary policy, and the government sets tax policy and, therefore, public investment priorities. Some decisions would have to be made centrally, as they affect the entire economy.

The benefit of socialism is that those decisions can be made democratically in the public interest, not by an oligarchy for the benefit of themselves. A truly democratic society can develop how the central planning will work, who will do the planning, who will approve the plan, how the community will voice its approval or disapproval of the plan, and what issues will be subject to the plan. It could also decide when central planning should override decisions made at the local or enterprise level and when it shouldn't.

If people are sophisticated enough to choose their own leaders and to operate an economy democratically, they are certainly sophisticated enough to design political controls to guard against planners using political or police power to become a self-perpetuating dictatorship. The planners would be democratically chosen, could only serve for limited terms, and would have no power outside their office. We can avoid the emergence of a new oligarchy by ensuring that incomes will vary only within a very narrow range.

With capitalism, the system's success supposedly comes from the interplay of the profit motive and the market—with, of course, a big helping hand from the government, including taxation to pay for the infrastructure, education, police, military, courts, coinage, and the various regulatory agencies. So what would replace the profit motive and the market?

First, the profit motive. Can humans cooperate, or must they compete to succeed? Is it true that the prospect of amassing a huge fortune is necessary to motivate people to spend the necessary time and effort studying and/or training to develop and perfect their art, profession, or creative genius? Was that the motivation for J. S. Bach, Isaac Newton, Albert Einstein, or Jesse Owens?

The geniuses whose innovations underlie whatever progress we have made have not been the capitalists. At best, entrepreneurs have organized production based on the discoveries of those who were motivated by scientific curiosity and had the time to study, explore, and develop their ideas. In fact, many, if not most, of the innovations of the twentieth century were developed by the military or public universities. It was never necessary to turn those discoveries and innovations over to large corporations. The profits those corporations reaped rightfully belong to the taxpayers who paid the salaries and provided the laboratories for the people who actually made the discoveries and developed the technology.

If researchers were properly supported, whether individuals or small groups, working alone or in public universities or research labs, there is no reason why they couldn't continue to invent more efficient or more desirable products and/or methods of production. Nor is there any reason why a democratically run economy wouldn't take advantage of such developments. In fact, an economy based on worker-owned and -operated firms and a democratically controlled central plan would have more freedom to utilize new technology for the common good than an economy run by giant corporations and banks wedded to a particular business model.

Even so, wouldn't there be too many slackers if everyone were ensured that their needs would be met? Will people work efficiently without a boss wielding the lash of unemployment and starvation? Will a democratic socialist economy have to wait until humans become saintlike?

The answer to those questions is no. There is empirical evidence from worker-owned and controlled firms that people who are actually invested in an enterprise will work harder, more efficiently, and more cooperatively. There is no historical evidence of a society collapsing because its people refused to do what was necessary to survive—that is, to work. Is it really conceivable that a democratically run economy would fail because too many people would refuse to act responsibly and go to work, or that they would democratically vote to starve to death?

In a democratically run economy it might be necessary, even desirable, to give people additional compensation or time off to study or train, or for performing onerous or dangerous work. A democratic economy is certainly capable of solving these compensation issues, whether at the firm level or the national level, without creating a new class of privileged individuals who could undermine the democratic basis of the economy.

The mobilization for World War II proved Americans' ability to cooperate for a social good they believed in. Surely a cooperative economy that delivers a decent life would be an equally strong motivation, even without the death and destruction of war. In today's unfair society, most people go to work, act responsibly, and feel empathy for their fellow citizens. There is no reason to believe that an economy operated by the people and for the people would have fewer responsible and productive citizens.

How about the market? What's going to ensure that resources, including labor, are utilized efficiently, and that the right mix of products and services is produced?

In theory, in the classic Adam Smith model, a free-market society does this when numerous equally powerful producers compete to supply the demand at the lowest cost and consumers can seek out the best product at the lowest price. In reality, capitalists and the profit motive produce monopolies and oligopolies that gain enough power to distort the market. The market, despite being regulated by government to a significant extent, doesn't do such a great job, given the amount of waste, duplication, environmental destruction, and harmful products it produces, and the gross disparities in income and wealth that it causes.

If not markets, then what? How will firms decide what to produce, and at what price? The answer is the same one now used by corporations: customer surveys and computer-generated plans. In today's world of electronic communication, economic units can make pretty good estimates of how many cars, shirts, rolls of toilet paper, or tons of steel to produce. If they are wrong, they can correct the error as efficiently, if not more efficiently, than private, profit-oriented corporations. And experience may demonstrate that there is a place for a market in a democratic, socialist economy—perhaps for local farmers, small businesses, and services like plumbers, tailors, and hairdressers. If so, that issue can be decided democratically. There are no inherent or insurmountable barriers to a democratic economy running efficiently, equitably, and environmentally responsibly *without* capitalists.

There are, of course, many other issues. How will work be distributed? Who will do the undesirable work? Who will do the desirable work? How will wages and salaries be determined? Who should play what role in controlling the workplace—workers, labor unions, political parties, the community? All of these important issues can be resolved democratically. We don't need a group of oligarchs or capitalism itself to do that. Nor does the difficulty of resolving them imply that creating a democratically run economy is infeasible, undesirable—unnecessary.

A democratic socialist society can also correct itself in ways capitalism can't. It was evident long before 2007 that the housing boom and therefore the economy were headed for disaster. But the capitalist system failed to remedy these problems before the crash, just as it failed to correct similar imbalances that caused the Great Depression. Nor can we implement even the most obvious solutions for the environmental crisis and the shortage of health care, because capitalism's interests oppose anything that would diminish the fortunes these interests make from the status quo.

This problem will not go away entirely in a democratic socialist economy. Some people or groups may be reluctant to change the way they work. But they will not have the power to block solutions obvious to the majority. The solutions to problems likely to arise in any economy are best addressed by applying the best evidence and the best intelligence to a means of sharing costs and, of course, benefits.

The evidence is that a democratically run socialist economy could function competently and equitably, and that it could provide essential goods, services, and economic security to the entire population. That is the economy we must have. The world can no longer sustain the ecologically destructive, wasteful, and inhumane capitalist system and its distorted allocation of privilege and wealth.

We can create this alternative economy and society if we have the courage to fight together to achieve it.

Chapter 4

The Shape of a Post-Capitalist Future

Rick Wolff

Since 2007, capitalism has mired most of the world in a deepening crisis: unemployment, stagnant or declining wages, reduced job benefits and security, and rising poverty. Government policies and reforms to stop this economic decline have failed either because they were inadequate or because they actually made things worse by reducing public employment and services in the name of "austerity." The "recovery" was limited to a small group of corporations, rich investors, and the stock markets they dominate—and even that recovery has now sputtered out.

The number of capitalism's critics is increasing rapidly, but most people seem persuaded that a workable socialist alternative is no longer feasible. The notion that socialism doesn't work or isn't relevant is widespread, especially since the Soviet system's collapse twenty-odd years ago. Nor do the conditions of contemporary China, however conducive to GDP growth, challenge that persuasion. This lack of a powerful, attractive, and credible vision of socialism is a major block to social movements against capitalism, despite the inequality, waste, and suffering that system has produced.

To conceive an alternative, we need to look at how capitalism organizes the internal workings of corporations—the enterprises that now produce most of the system's goods and services. Capitalism's organization of production—and especially the exploitation it builds on—drives the decisions made by those who run capitalist enterprises. Their decisions shape the economic development and also the politics and culture of modern society. Yet socialists' critiques of capitalism over the last century have rarely focused on transforming that internal organization—which shapes how capitalism works or fails to work—to eliminate the exploitation it engenders.

Corporate boards of directors are crucial to modern capitalism and, therefore, to exploitation. They are its key decision-makers. This follows from their position as the appropriators of the "surplus value" produced by its laborers—the value the workers add by their labor minus the wages paid to them. Corporate boards use part of that appropriated surplus to expand the enterprise and accumulate capital, another part to pay their managers, another to pay dividends to their shareholders, still another to fund the politicians, parties, universities, and think tanks that shape policies and public opinion, and so on.

Capitalist corporations typically display a basic four-part internal structure. At the top is the board of directors, usually comprised of fifteen to twenty people. They hire the workers and managers, receive the gross revenues from sales of the company's output, determine what to produce and where and how to produce it, and decide how to utilize or distribute the net revenues, including profits.

The corporation's major shareholders—its chief owners—are the second part. They select the members of the board of directors and also influence how (to whom and for what) the board distributes the surplus it appropriates. The third part includes the workers who directly produce the goods and services sold by the corporation. The fourth part is "auxiliary" or "indirect" workers: the managers and supervisors, clerks, and others who create the framework for the workers to produce profitably—the ones who buy the supplies, sell the products, and do administrative and support work.

Essentially, one group of people, the direct workers, produces surplus value, enriching the enterprise beyond what they're paid. Another group, the board of directors, appropriates and distributes that surplus value; all workers are excluded from that appropriation and distribution. The relationship of workers who produce and directors who appropriate surplus value defines capitalist exploitation.

Socialists, however, have struggled chiefly to change *other* aspects of capitalist societies, especially their typical systems of property ownership and their mechanisms for distributing productive resources and output. Traditionally, socialists assumed that the transition from capitalism to socialism would entail moving enterprises from private to social or national ownership and relying on government planning instead of the market to determine how to distribute goods and services.

Socialists thus wanted to end, or at least sharply reduce, the private ownership of the means of production (land, factories, tools and equipment, stores, offices, etc.) and to substitute socialized or nationalized property. In the name and service of the entire population, the state would become the owner of the productive property and thereby establish a post-capitalist society. In practice, this often meant that the state would use those means of production within state-owned and state-operated enterprises. In more moderate scenarios, the state might share ownership with private persons and groups or make socialized property available to private enterprises under lease, rental, or shareholding arrangements.

Socialists traditionally wanted to stop relying on markets as the chief mechanism for distributing productive resources and outputs (goods and services) among enterprises, workers, and consumers. They criticized the market for entrenching fundamental economic, political, and cultural inequalities. They blamed the market for the profound instability of capitalism, for its socially wasteful business cycles that repeatedly produced recessions and unemployment, bankruptcy, and home foreclosures.

Socialists advocated planning (by centralized or decentralized political authorities) to limit or abolish markets. In practice, this often meant using social criteria to regulate, control, or determine commodity prices in market exchanges. Some wanted to dispense with markets and prices altogether and instead directly distribute resources and goods to producers and consumers according to a central plan that prioritized social needs and goals.

Indeed, socialism came to be widely understood as an alternative to capitalism that substituted socialized property and planning for private property and markets. Socialists did not pay much attention to the internal organization of enterprises. In the Soviet Union, for example, replacing capitalism with socialism meant state ownership of the means of production and running the economy by central planning instead of through private property and markets.

Soviet state enterprises largely retained the basic four-part capitalist organizational system. Instead of corporate boards of directors, a council of ministers reserved for itself the same basic decisions. As in a capitalist corporation, the council was a different group of people from those doing the direct work of producing goods and services—so the relationship between it and those direct workers was also exploitative. Instead of private shareholders choosing a board of directors, the Soviet government and Communist Party selected the members of the council of ministers and influenced its distribution of the surpluses that it appropriated from state enterprises. Finally, the council basically hired the enterprise's workers.

This combination of capitalistically organized enterprises with socialized property and central planning led some socialists to say that the economies of the Soviet Union and the People's Republic of China were not really socialist, but rather a kind of state capitalism.

Either way, what collapsed two decades ago was the exploitative system in the Soviet Union and most of Eastern Europe. The similarly exploitative system in the People's Republic of China did not collapse. Instead, it generated the world's fastest GDP growth over the last two decades. In any case, that system did not and does not represent the only model of socialism.

Another model of the socialist alternative to capitalism would focus on the internal organization of enterprises and insist on a radically different way of organizing the production, appropriation, and distribution of the enterprise's surplus and of making the major decisions governing the enterprise's activities.

In capitalist corporations, the board of directors, with input from the larger stockholders, appropriates and distributes the surplus value produced by the direct workers. By contrast, in democratically organized socialist enterprises, the direct workers would function collectively as the board of directors, strongly influenced by the auxiliary workers. Instead of workers (the majority) being ruled and exploited by boards and major shareholders—a small minority—the workers would make the crucial economic decisions and decide how to distribute the money their work brought in.

They would share this decision-making power with the residential communities whose lives are interdependent with their enterprises. These groups would have to negotiate, design, and adjust how their shared decision-making would work. The residents of the surrounding neighborhood might have more say on issues such as noise and traffic generated by the workplace, but the workers would have more say on internal issues such as their own schedules; different socialist enterprises will display a variety of such arrangements.

The democratic socialization of work—centered on the elimination of exploitation—deserves to be a major component of an alternative socialist vision of a post-capitalist future. Work—the deliberate application of mind and body to producing objects or services that we need and want—is central to sustaining any society; it is also central to people's quality of life. Whatever the benefits of socialized property and planning relative to private property and markets, they do not guarantee that the organization of work will be different from what it is under capitalism. When state enterprises position state officials as the appropriators and distributors of the surpluses produced by other people, capitalist exploitation has not been eliminated. Rather, state capitalist exploitation has replaced private capitalist exploitation.

The history of twentieth-century socialism in the Soviet Union, China, and elsewhere illustrates what can happen when the way "socialist" enterprises are organized retains its capitalist four-part division. The tensions, oppositions, and struggles that division created eventually undermined those societies' socialization of property and economic planning. Exploitation left intact inside state enterprises can work to convert them into private enterprises and dismantle planning in favor of markets.

In the alternative model of socialism emphasized here, enterprises might, for example, split their workweeks into two parts. Workers would do their regular jobs from Monday through Thursday. They would not necessarily always have one specific task; the old socialist idea of rotating jobs among individuals could be readily accommodated. On Fridays, all direct workers would meet to appropriate and distribute the surpluses (thereby eliminating exploitation). The auxiliary workers and community residents would join them to decide democratically who will receive what portions of the surplus and to make all the other basic decisions: what, how, and where to produce; how long the workday and workweek will be; and so on.

Socialist enterprises organized in these ways would make decisions systematically different from those of capitalist enterprises. They would be much less likely to relocate production across the country or the globe, to use technologies that harm their workers' or neighbors' health, to spend money bulking up on intrusive supervisory staff, or to permit the extreme inequalities in remuneration between direct workers and top managers that now typify capitalist enterprises. Socialist enterprises would be far *more* likely to use the money they bring in to enhance the lives of workers (via child care, elder care, and medical and educational programs) and to prepare, retrain, and reposition workers to respond to changes in technology or in the demand for what they produce.

When these socialist enterprises distribute their surplus, their objectives would include workers' well-being but no longer include profits and growth for the small minority of owners. When these socialist enterprises pay taxes, their demands regarding how governments use those taxes will reflect the workers' wants, needs, and ideas rather than those of the small minority of boards and major shareholders.

In traditional capitalist economies, profit, capital accumulation, and enlarging corporations' market shares are prioritized over community and social needs. Corporate boards of directors and major shareholders have incentives to enforce those priorities and control the resources to do so. They usually prefer not to devote resources to day-care centers for children, limits on pollution, productive programs for the elderly, and educational facilities available to everyone lifelong. When workers and community residents together decide how to distribute surpluses, they will make different decisions.

By democratically reorganizing their internal structures and operations to eliminate exploitation, socialist enterprises will begin a transition from today's so-called democracy to the real thing. Workers who democratically design and direct their enterprises will likely demand parallel democratic participation in their communities' governance. Likewise, community residents who have the power to influence enterprise decisions will better understand the compromises needed to balance the society's economic needs with its other priorities.

In capitalist enterprises, workers are excluded from virtually all basic enterprise decisions. Their skills, aptitudes, and disposition for such activities erode, and that undermines their interest in and concern for the enterprise's development. That alienation from participation and responsibility inside enterprises also infects political, civic, and community life. Most appeals to working people to participate in politics go unanswered. The absence of democratic participation where we work sustains that apathy; a transition to workers' self-directed enterprises could cure it.

That transition would also transform cultural life. For example, there would no longer be a set of elite institutions (mostly expensive private boarding schools, colleges, and universities) exclusively for training the leaders of industry and ranked and privileged above second-tier schools (in the "better suburbs") that train managers. Nor would there be a bottom level (vocational, technical, or "inner city" schools and community colleges) for workers, drudges, and order-takers, those assigned to jobs without any authority or influence in the design or direction of their workplaces. When all workers have to participate in running their enterprises, they will need and demand correspondingly integrated and comprehensive educations at schools where what is taught, how it is taught, and what resources are provided to support teaching are equal.

The cultural norms, tastes, and pursuits of Americans will be democratized, and much of the discrimination summarized by terms like "high" and "low" culture will atrophy. Opera, many forms of painting, and fencing, for example, will no longer be appreciated by, accessible to, and engaged in only by the usual class-based minorities. With productive wealth socialized, gaps between high and low incomes will narrow, and schooling will be less compromised by deep economic and social divisions. As their own boards of directors, workers, in a democratic partnership with residential communities, would take a significant step toward genuine equality of opportunity that would otherwise remain mere rhetoric.

A post-capitalist future can be built upon a foundation of democratizing enterprises. They represent real alternatives to capitalism. A better world is possible: the United States can do better than capitalism.

The economic crisis of the early twenty-first century has revealed the immense failures of the capitalist system. It has inspired ever more Americans to think about alternatives and pursue them. Imagine the possibilities of a revived, unified movement that mobilizes these people.

Chapter 5

Law in a Socialist USA

Michael Steven Smith

"I won't sit at the dinner table with nothing on my plate and call myself a diner."

—Malcolm X

"Land of the brave, home of the free, I don't want to be mistreated by no bourgeoisie."

—Lead Belly

What would law be like if we didn't have capitalism in America, if we replaced it and were able to live in a genuinely socialist society? Imagine a society of ecological sanity, material abundance, and social equality; a society where social relations are premised on human solidarity, not capitalist exploitation and human competition; where people are not set against each other; where production for profit, driven by private greed and accumulation of capital, has given way to production for public use.

To envision what the law would become, we need to understand where it came from. Law is not a fixed system but an evolving one, bound up with changing social conditions. The law we have now—contracts, property, corporate, trusts and estates, domestic relations, torts (injuries) —is based on the ownership of private property (corporations and banks, not toothbrushes). But it wasn't always that way.

A thousand years ago, Europe was a feudal society with different social conditions and different laws. Feudal society was static. Land ownership was frozen in relatively wealthy, propertied families. Trade and commerce were confined to luxury goods for the rich. Charging of interest on loans was forbidden, thereby inhibiting commerce and banking. Life centered around isolated villages and the large manor houses of the nobility. Most people were serfs, semi-slaves bound for life to an aristocratic ruler. How did this change into what we have now?

The modern bourgeoisie, or ruling class, or the "1 percent" as the Occupy movement famously describes them, started off as part of the 99 percent. They began their long march to power as humble merchants in medieval Europe. They were the early capitalists in what was then a feudal society. The law they created and refined over the years is the law we live under today. (Legal scholars Michael Tigar and Madeleine R. Levy pioneered the study of the history of the law which they developed in their book *Law and the Rise of Capitalism*.)

These bourgeois revolutionaries brought about a newly dominant legal ideology based upon a different system of social relations. They sought old legal forms—mainly Roman—and invested them with a new commercial content. They also used canon (church) law, royal law, feudal law, and "natural law" (common sense) to construct a socially protected system of commerce as well as to promote, and thereby profit more from, advances in technology.

In pursuit of their material interests, the bourgeoisie established the freedom of contract, with the ability to sell land and to lend and borrow money with interest. They devised laws to regulate all this, courts to adjudicate disputes, and a central power to enforce their judgments. These were all preconditions for the growth of modern society. In large measure, the medieval bourgeoisie and their lawyers prepared the way for today's possibility of abundance.

Significant legal change is the product of conflict between social classes seeking to turn the institutions of social control to their own purposes and to impose and maintain a specific system of socioeconomic relations. The transformation from the legal system in feudal times took some 800 years. The rising bourgeoisie couldn't buy property freely in a real-estate market or associate politically or economically. They were social outcasts whose profit-taking was thought to be dishonorable, a form of usury that put their souls in jeopardy. Called *pies poudreuse*, or dusty feet, they peddled their goods from market to town to fair.

But this disreputable lot first accommodated to, then openly confronted, and finally overthrew the legal ideology of feudalism. They subordinated and sacrificed all of feudalism's ties of personal fealty and hierarchy to capitalism's bonds of cash and contract. The Enlightenment French philosopher Denis Diderot described the mode of their progress: "The strange god settles himself humbly on the altar beside the god of the country. Little by little he establishes himself firmly. Then one fine morning he gives his neighbor a shove with his elbow and crash!—the idol lies upon the ground."

After accumulating for centuries in the feudal formations, capitalist law cataclysmically replaced feudal law in the English and French revolutions of the seventeenth and eighteenth centuries. This historical precedent can help us understand how the law will change again to reflect different property relations in the transition to socialism.

Karl Marx and Friedrich Engels put forward what subsequently became known as the commodity theory of law. Marx identified the material premises of our prevailing legal relations and set them forth in his book *Capital*. The legal system, swollen with codes, courts, law schools, law-making bodies, publications, and prisons is based on transactions bound up with the production of articles for exchange, money, and the rights of private property. Under capitalism's system of generalized commodity production, individuals became legal subjects having rights, especially contractual rights to buy and sell commodities—including the power of labor, which itself is a commodity. The buyer and the seller exchange equivalents, things that are equal in value. Law regulates this exchange, and the state enforces the law.

An equal standard is applied. No allowance is made for the natural inequality of individual talent. As Marx wrote, "A given amount of labor in one form is exchanged for an equal amount of labor in another form." However, he concluded, that bourgeois right, embedded in market relations, is superficial and formal. The social and economic inequalities between the classes restrict and negate it.

In this system, the ruling minority of the rich monopolize the means of production, while the working people are dispossessed. In order to live, they must sell their labor power to a boss at the prevailing wage rates. This transaction, which conforms to the rules of the market and the legal code, appears fair to both sides. But it really masks a relation of inequality, because workers produce more value in the process of production than they are paid for. That is the source of their exploitation. Bourgeois law justifies this unjust state of affairs.

Since commodity relations will continue to persist in the United States as we make the transition from capitalism to socialism, our laws will continue to reflect bourgeois norms, however mitigated, because of unavoidable inequalities. The state and the law it upholds will eventually become unnecessary when there is an abundance of goods and the individual exchange of equivalents through the market becomes unnecessary. Even now, in our capitalist society, we see a glimpse of the future in employee stock-ownership programs, the 48,000 cooperatives that market 30 percent of all farm produce, and in publicly owned banks, life-insurance companies, electric and water companies, hospitals, cable TV stations, and Internet providers.

In a rationally, democratically organized society that has done away with capitalist private property, which is used only to produce for profit and not for human needs, that day will come fairly soon. Legal institutions as we know them, and the juridical element in social relations, must gradually disappear as commodity relations die out.

The rule will become "from each according to their ability, to each according to their need." There will be no need for law as we know it. Human relations will become regulated more by custom, as they once were before the advent of class society.

Law in America is sold as an impartial force for justice and equality. Its origins are shrouded in mystery and invested with the sanction of tradition. Most people have trouble buying this proposition, as indicated by the public-opinion polls that find lawyers to be the second-most unpopular group of professionals in the country, just behind politicians. The fraudulence of the formal equality of rights and the apparent neutrality of judges was brilliantly pierced by Anatole France's oft-quoted remark— that the law in all its majesty forbids all persons, whether rich or poor, from sleeping under bridges.

With socialism in America, the people will own the bridges, and they'll sleep peacefully and contentedly with a roof over their heads knowing that they have created a society in which the law won't work against them and, in the words of the great Communist Manifesto, "where the free development of each is the condition of the free development of all."

Chapter 6

Alternatives to the Present System of Capitalist Injustice

Mumia Abu-Jamal and Angela Davis

We live in an era of mega-incarceration on a scale that can scarcely be imagined. The United States locks up more of its people than any other nation in the world. About 2.3 million Americans presently call prison or jail cells home—almost five times as many as there were in 1980. More than 60 percent of these prisoners are Black or Latino, according to the Sentencing Project. With another five million people on probation or parole, almost one out of every 30 American adults is under some form of correctional supervision.

Moreover, jails and prisons in the United States have become venues of profit as well as of punishment. As the number of inmates has expanded, private prison corporations have become significant players both here and in the international market. State-owned and state-operated prisons have outsourced services to private companies, diminishing the difference between private and public prisons.

Any sober investigation into the American criminal justice system leads inescapably to the conclusion that it is unfair, unjust, dysfunctional, unbalanced, and profoundly expensive—both in societal and human terms. How it got that way has less to do with criminality and more with sociopolitical and economic factors, for who goes to prison is inevitably related to the role that the economic and political elites assign to persons in this society—by who shall exploit whom.

Any serious attempt to arrive at solutions thus has to move beyond both capitalism and its systems of retributive (punishment-based) justice. Over the last decade or so, a mass movement targeting what activists call the "prison-industrial complex" has taken shape. In 2011, the NAACP released a report, "Misplaced Priorities: Over Incarcerate Under Educate," that linked the decline in the quality of education with the soaring prison population.

Initially, though, we must consider the terms we are using, for the concept of "crime," like much that we today take for granted, is a sociopolitical construct.

In the 1970s, "radical criminologists called the legal definition of crime into question and thereby opened to doubt the very scope of the field of criminology," scholar David F. Greenberg wrote. Herman and Julia Schwendinger, he noted, "argued that to restrict research to violations of state-made law is to accept the definitions of harm and wrongfulness that the state asserts, and they urged their coworkers to redefine crime as a violation of human rights. These definitions are based on the conceptions of harm held by those who have the power to make law, and consequently tend to exclude from scrutiny harms caused by the actions of the upper class."

The American Friends Service Committee's Working Party expressed the spirit with which radical criminologists rejected official definitions. "Actions that clearly ought to be labeled 'criminal,' because they bring the greatest harm to the greatest number, are in fact accomplished officially by agencies of the government," it stated in 1971.

The overwhelming number of murders in this century has been committed by governments in wartime. Hundreds of unlawful killings by police go unreported each year. The largest forceful acquisitions of property in the United States have been the theft of lands guaranteed by treaty to Indian tribes, thefts sponsored by the government. The largest number of dislocations, tantamount to kidnapping—the evacuation and internment of Japanese-Americans during World War II—were carried out by the government with the approval of the courts. Civil rights demonstrators, struggling to exercise their constitutional rights, have been repeatedly beaten and harassed by police and sheriffs. And in the Vietnam War, America has violated its Constitution and international law.

Social structures—courts, police, prisons, and so on—have within them a deep bias about what constitutes crime and what does not. Any social structure is a product of its previous historical, economic, and social iterations, and these previous forms significantly influence later forms. The present system, in addition to being increasingly repressive, is the logical inheritance of its racist, hierarchical, exploitative past—a reactive formation to attempts to transform, democratize, and socialize it.

For authentic democracy to emerge, "abolition democracy" must be enacted—the abolition of institutions that advance the dominance of any one group over any other. It is the democracy that is possible if we continue the legacy of the great abolition movements in American history, those that opposed slavery, lynching, and segregation. As long as the prison-industrial complex remains, American democracy will continue to be a false one. Such a false democracy reduces people and their communities to the barest biological subsistence because it pushes them outside the law and the polity.

The idea of abolition democracy comes from a reading of US history in which the freedom struggle is central to who Americans are and to *why* we are who we are. We are less exemplars of legendary "Founding Fathers" than we are of "founding freedom fighters"—inheritors of those who fought for their freedom, not from a British aristocracy, but from American slavocracy.

We need to prepare not only a critique of a repressive, incarceral status quo, but a vision of a new, enlightened, more humane, more socialized view of a future without mass incarceration.

The rise of the prison-industrial complex and the mass incarceration of African Americans is the most recent incarnation of how human bondage and racial repression—the American way of life for two-thirds of its national existence—strive to reassert themselves, albeit via different faces and forms.

The Union's victory over the Confederacy in the Civil War and the ratification of the Thirteenth, Fourteenth, and Fifteenth Amendments to the Constitution during Reconstruction spelled slavery's doom. Within a few years, however, the system thought buried by war was exhumed and given new life under the program of leasing convicts as labor. It was slavery in every sense but its name. Indeed, as it was public instead of private slavery, it was in some ways worse. With a new face, to be sure, but the same bite, the same hungers, the same skewed consciousness, the golem of stolen labor lived again, this time as a fixture of the prison system, which, through notorious Black Codes and police targeting of Black communities, consigned generations of Black men and women to endless lives of toil and state terror, in service of corporate profits.

For these many, many people, freedom was but a poor and cruel joke. And the peonage system that succeeded slavery kept millions of others in bondage. "Under the aegis of the Freedmen's Bureau, large numbers of black peasants signed annual contracts with white planters," the esteemed Black scholars Mary Frances Berry and John W. Blassingame wrote in *Long Memory* in 1982. "Generally penniless, they obtained advances on their wages or shares of the crop. Since they were illiterate, the planters often overcharged and cheated them. The result was perpetual debt, compulsion, violence, oppression, and de facto slavery. The murder of black peons was a frequent occurrence in the 1940s."

In 1907, a white resident of Florida argued, "Slavery is just as much an 'institution' now as it was before the war." The Georgia Baptist Convention agreed with this view in 1939: "There are more negroes held by these debt slavers than were actually owned as slaves before the War Between the States." A federal anti-peonage law was passed in 1948, under pressure from the activism of US communists, and peonage complaints were filed with the Justice Department well into the 1970s.

What sociologist Loic Wacquant has termed the "penal state" is driving the profound social inequality and unparalleled repression that is the prison-industrial complex. Economic, political, and social forces have converged to create a system of vested interests to ensure its continued expansion and wealth.

In sum, the present system drains public resources to pursue a chimera of public safety when it is actually a legalized system of violence against unprivileged communities, who have been the historical bogeymen of the American body politic. It is, too, a retort against the alleged goal of social justice, and is a profound waste of human potential and social development.

With less than 5 percent of the world's population, how comes it that the United States has around 25 percent of the world's prison population? That is a sign of imbalance, not an exemplar of social justice.

We have stated the problems. It is time to proffer some solutions.

Socialist Alternatives?

How can we transform institutions such as the prison in ways that are inspired by visions of socialism? From where are we to draw models or alternatives to the present system, especially in an era when the socialist community is in such disarray, if not full retreat? Russia? Cuba? China? Albania?

Implicit in such a question is the assumption that external models are the only ones available to us, and that no such internal model exists.

This is a fractured view of the nation's history, for, to quote James Baldwin, "American history is longer, more various, more beautiful, and more terrible than anything anyone has ever said about it. "

The US federal system—a kind of dual sovereignty—owes much to the Iroquois Confederacy, or the Six Nations Confederacy, which comprised the Mohawk, Oneida, Onondaga, Cayuga, Seneca, and Tuscarora nations. The confederacy lasted for several centuries despite enormous pressure from the Anglo-Americans.

The indigenous peoples of this continent, according to some historians, gave far better evidence of democracy, gender equality, and racism-free life and governance than its European invaders did. We might also discover important insights about justice by looking at histories of indigenous people. Among the Native Americans of the Northeast, criminal justice was a communal concern.

"No laws or ordinances, sheriffs and constables, judges and juries, or courts or jails—the apparatus of authority in European societies—were to be found in the Northeast woodlands prior to European arrival. Yet boundaries of acceptable behavior were firmly set. Though priding themselves on the autonomous individual, the Iroquois maintained a strict sense of right and wrong," historian Gary Nash noted in his groundbreaking work

Red, White, and Black: The Peoples of Early America. "He who stole another's food or acted invalourously in war was 'shamed' by his people and ostracized from their company until he had atoned for his actions and demonstrated to their satisfaction that he had morally purified himself."

In other words, respect for individuality did not have to lead to modes of punishment that separated the individual from the community both physically and symbolically. "The Western way is to punish you, so that you don't repeat the behavior," Robert Yazzie, former chief justice of the Navajo Nation Supreme Court, told the International Institute for Restorative Practices in 2004. "But the Navajo way is to focus on the individual. You separate the action from the person." This approach points to a form of justice that does not rely on the assumption that the quality of the harm created by a person can be translated into quantitative terms, such as a specific length of prison time.

The Navajo peacemaking process, Yazzie said, brings the offender and the victim together to talk to each other.

> *The first order of business the relatives would do in the peacemaking process is to get to the bottom of a problem. In court, I would sue you for battery and the state would say we have to prove all the elements of a crime and use the rules or the law to prove that you are guilty . . . that's beside the point. What matters here is: why did this act happen in the first place? There's a reason why the harm has occurred. Let's deal with that. Maybe we have a history of problems between the two of us. If we can get to the bottom of a problem, all the other stuff will fall into place. The damage can be acknowledged by you, and I can go away happy from the process, knowing that you say that you're not going to do it again.*

This form of justice may be unobtainable in contemporary American society, but it contains much less oppression and torture than the Anglo-American form, and it takes a profoundly different approach. It is not a form of justice without pain. In a traditional society, being ostracized would be the greatest disability, for individuals' self-definition relied, in great part, upon their membership and place within the clan and the tribe—the community. These people knew one another and thus were best able to determine how to respond to violations of communal well-being. They modeled the road not taken.

Yet their very existence shows us the powerful historical precedents that can inform our present by fueling a bigger, broader, deeper definition of America, one that is centered on freedom rather than domination, one that is more nation than empire.

Establishing community courts (especially ones composed of non-lawyers) would utilize these insights from traditional societies and thus mitigate the destructiveness inherent in the present corporate-type, assembly-line system that is breaking state budgets and individuals' bodies and spirits on the anvil of so-called criminal justice.

Nor is this idea unthinkable within the current US legal system. In Pennsylvania, both the state constitution and state law provide for the establishment of "community courts" as a section of what's termed the minor judiciary. One was opened in Philadelphia in 2002, becoming one of approximately thirty community courts in US cities (and fifty outside the United States). Like its counterparts, the Philadelphia Community Court was empowered to use community service and other restorative sanctions to address "quality of life" offenses such as prostitution, drug possession, and theft.

When the court closed down in September 2011 due to funding cuts, it had enabled more than 500,000 hours of community service. It also provided offenders with social services such as medical care and drug counseling.

"The whole purpose of community court was to take a holistic approach and to kind of address the needs of the individuals as they came in, with the recognition that sometimes people found themselves in court with issues that went beyond the case that was presented to the judge," Municipal Court President Judge Marsha Neifield told the *Philadelphia Weekly*.

"Community justice represents not a simple return to the rehabilitative ideal, but an approach to crime and punishment that is radically different from that of the traditional criminal justice process," Adriaan Lanni wrote in the *Harvard Civil Rights-Civil Liberties Law Review* in 2005. "Community justice initiatives—which include community prosecution, community courts, sentencing circles, and citizen reparative boards—advocate local, decentralized crime control policies generated through widespread citizen participation. They emphasize attacking the causes of crime, rehabilitating individual offenders, and repairing the harm caused by crime rather than punishing offenders according to traditional retributive or deterrent concerns."

Community courts that have attempted to use non-retributive or restorative justice models implicitly resist the mechanics of capitalist justice. They can demonstrate that it is far more effective to try to transform the social relations that have been damaged by those who commit acts of harm against others than to rely on prison sentences. Thus these courts can serve as an important fulcrum for challenging and providing alternatives to retributive justice—which, combined with the criminalization of Black and Latino communities, has led to a titanic increase in the numbers of people behind bars.

It is the principle of non-retributive justice that is important here, for it illustrates exactly how feasible this suggestion is.

Freedom in one's communal life can bleed into the community's economic life, especially as the national polity forms structures that reflect its political will.

Thus a nonracist community, which is theoretically free of the ideological blinders and bondage of white supremacy, could create social policies that conform more to the innate humanity of all persons, rather than to the exploitation of fear that typifies the regnant structures of criminal justice.

What, systemically, must be changed?

If we see the present structure as problematic, then we must consider how to destroy, reconstruct, or ameliorate it. And if history is our guide, we must be vigorous, for else we will see old forms reassert themselves with new masks, protecting the same (or worse) inequalities.

What we decide to do will be open to the decisions of popular, democratic groupings in the future as they seek greater humanistic and socialistic expressions, but a basic preliminary list would include:

- End mass incarceration by prison abolition.
- Abolish the death penalty.
- Establish communal courts.
- Make education a constitutional and human right.
- Make human needs more primary than property rights.

It's also time to end the racist "war on drugs," which is as illogical as it is ineffective. It has been little more than a mask for massing state power against social movements and lower-class populations.

We cannot, at this juncture of history, pussyfoot around.

The cynical among us might well say, "Humph! That's all fine and dandy. But how do you get there from here?"

Fair question.

Those of us who have lived in, worked in, and studied history know that social change is no short-term or ready-made process. We know that social movements play a decisive role in that process, for they move nations from one seemingly settled place to quite other places over time.

As repression continues, so too must resistance. Abolition democracy is one vision of how to deepen and extend that resistance. A central tenet of it is building (or perhaps rebuilding) movements of prisoners and movements against mass incarceration. The movement to abolish slavery, which many activists cite today in the prison context, was a bold and daring project. Those resolute men and women transformed America by fighting for social change and refusing to submit to a slavocracy.

The great abolitionist (and ex-slave) Frederick Douglass captured this theme brilliantly when he said, "If there is no struggle, there is no progress."

Chapter 7

Socialism Is the Highest Expression of Human Rights

Ajamu Baraka

"Economic socialism without a communist morale does not interest me. We are fighting poverty, but at the same time alienation. . . . If communism is dissociated from conscious-ness, it may be a method of distribution, but it is no longer a revolutionary morality."

—Che Guevara

"The master's tools will never dismantle the master's house."

—Audre Lorde

What would socialism look like in the United States? What would a socialist movement look like? It would require a much broader concept of human rights than the one commonly held today.

One of the most contradictory elements of capitalist phi-losophy is its glorification of the abstract individual while real individuals and collectives are degraded and destroyed by capi-talism's imperialism and exploitation. The right-wing definition of "human rights" is primarily property rights, the right to make

71

money. The conventional liberal definition is limited to the rights of individuals to participate in the political process and to be protected against some types of discrimination.

The people-centered definition of human rights is those life-affirming rights that individuals and collectives define and secure for themselves through social struggle that express the highest commitment to human dignity and social justice for themselves and all humanity. We will not have these human rights without socialism, and we will not have socialism without these human rights.

Global capitalism and colonialism deny individuals and communities autonomy over their lives, resources, and histories; create and perpetuate systems of domination in every aspect of social life; and demean and distort the humanity of people. Therefore, the human-rights struggle must be anti-capitalist and anti-colonial. But those of us fighting from the margins for a new reality must also develop an alternative vision based on the highest ethical principles of societal organization and be committed to eliminating all forms of oppression. That means socialism. Human rights would be grounded in the expressed needs of the majority of the people.

Why only under socialism? Because restoring dignity, individually and collectively, and institutionalizing it in the fabric of society—that is, in all social relationships—is at the center of both the people-centered human rights idea and of socialism.

However, simply changing our economic system will not automatically eliminate all oppressive relationships. It will not end the separation of "worthy" human beings from the "unworthy," elitism and mindless consumerism, hatred for the poor, and white-supremacist ideology. It will take vigilance and time to overcome these. Therefore, we will have to struggle for dignity, for individuals and collectives, in our daily lives.

The new social relations, institutions, and structures that we establish must reflect a commitment to comprehensive human rights. And because democracy is at the center of the socialist project, state processes, expenditures, and policies will represent the priorities the people agree on.

In contemporary capitalist society, there is no right to work or have a viable standard of living. In a socialist society, the human right to work with just and favorable pay would mean that everyone would have the right to a socially productive job, at a level of pay that lets them enjoy life and participate in the cultural life of their community. Clean, safe, and comprehensive transportation systems would enable workers to get to their places of employment. Free day care would be provided for all who needed it. The right to rest and leisure would be as important as the right to work, as it is also essential for people to enjoy life and participate in their communities.

Even more importantly, the right to work under socialism would also mean the right to own and control the product of one's labor; it would mean the elimination of alienated labor and exploitation.

The human right to health would not only mean the right to free, comprehensive health care but also the right to refuse having toxic waste dumps and other things that poison people and the Earth imposed on one's community. The right to education would mean free and comprehensive schooling through to the university level. Education would go beyond training people for employment and help them develop critical consciousness and an anti-oppression perspective so they are better able to control their own destinies.

The right to social security in a socialist society would not be limited to a retirement program that provides a poverty-level income to people who worked all their lives, most of whom don't have a private pension or any other source of income. It would mean the right to be free of social insecurity throughout our lives. Real social security means that the items necessary for a dignified life—food, water, clothing, housing, medical care, and all necessary services—will be guaranteed for everyone through the collective pooling of resources and the democratically determined distribution of those resources. From each according to their skills, to each according to their needs, is the guarantee for the human right to social security.

Because of the United States' colonial history, realizing the right to self-determination for indigenous people and oppressed nationalities might mean that the nation we know today would no longer exist, or would not exist in the same form. It would mean respect for decisions made by Chicanos and African Americans, as nationally oppressed peoples, about their relationship to the United States. Therefore, it could mean independence for Puerto Rico and freedom for the indigenous people of Hawaii and Alaska.

Anti-colonialism and the free association of peoples are longstanding socialist principles, no matter how they have been violated in actual socialist practice over the years. We must struggle to uphold this principle, even if the prospect of what decolonization might mean is disconcerting to those of us not indigenous to the territory referred to as the United States. Decolonization should not be seen as a metaphor but as a real process that dislodges white-supremacist, bourgeois settler power and resists any attempt to reimpose white supremacy under a different guise, no matter how progressive and revolutionary it claims to be.

We cannot afford the fiction of a nonpolitical, objective concept of human rights that, beneath the surface of universality, reaffirms individualism, rationalizations for market capitalism, and white-supremacist patriarchy. For us, the fight for human rights is a life-or-death struggle, with the future of our communities and peoples at stake. Through our lived experience we understand that capitalism denies individuals and collectives a voice and dignity in all spheres of social life; that is its nature. We believe that the full potential of the idea of human rights, grounded in the notion of the inherent dignity of every person and community, can be realized only through the construction of a socialist society based on a different set of ethics and social relationships.

Che Guevara understood that for socialism to succeed, it had to base itself on a new ethics—a higher morality that rejected the vulgar materialism of capitalist society and the economism that characterized most of the failed attempts at socialism in the twentieth century. For us, the core of that ethical system is the radical, people-centered idea of human rights that asserts without apology that only a *socialist* United States can create the conditions for real human rights.

Chapter 8

Personal, Emotional, and Sexual Life Without Capitalism

Harriet Fraad and Tess Fraad-Wolff

Imagine what America would be like if success were measured by efficiency in producing kindness to each other rather than efficiency in producing more profit for the rich. Imagine what relationships would be like if connections between people were as celebrated as the accumulation of money.

Within the capitalist system, there is no point in hiring anyone unless you are making much more money from their work than you are paying to them in salary. All decision-making power is taken from the employee who produced the wealth. That is "good" business. Democracy and sharing disappear.

Kindness or fairness is not even considered, never mind rewarded. Thus, a clever business school graduate may be highly paid for inventing gimmicks that disguise hidden charges in our phone bills, added charges for banking operations, or interest charges on credit card accounts. What does it do to human relationships when such a person is thought of as clever rather than sneaky and dishonest?

What does it do to human relationships when denying others what their work is worth and any say over the product of their work is the road to success? How does that kind of ethical practice at work affect our behavior outside our jobs? Imagine how we would feel if we were not cheated out of the full value of our work.

Imagine feeling safe. At present in the United States, "precarity" defines most of our work situations. It is considered efficient to lay people off and give little or no security to new workers. Workers never know when or how they might be laid off. Millions more work on freelance, temporary, or contract jobs and don't know where their next paycheck will come from when their current job ends. Precarity casts its shadow across our plans for the future and secure lives for families and children.

Imagine the luxury of time. Most European Union nations give workers four to six weeks of guaranteed paid leave for vacation. People get extra time off if they are sick. Imagine knowing you and your family and friends could have the time and space to get to know one another, to have the talks that can only happen when there is time and relaxation. Imagine counting on time to enjoy life.

Imagine having to work less than forty hours a week and still receive full benefits, or having flextime and being able to choose what hours you work.

Imagine the good feeling of having a job where the workers run their businesses together, cooperatively deciding what to produce, how to produce it, and what to do with the money they generate—as they do in Mondragon, an 85,000-member cooperative in Spain. If you visit Mondragon, you can't fail to notice the relaxed, kind way in which people interact.

Imagine not fearing layoffs! Democracy at work would prevent the terror of job insecurity that plagues Americans. Worker-run companies do not outsource their own jobs. In Mondragon, if there is a business slowdown, the workers decide how much to cut their pay and the hours they work. If the co-op's businesses must cut back more, workers are guaranteed jobs and retraining to work in a different Mondragon business. Imagine the health and mental health benefits for all if we were not so frightened of losing our jobs.

In democratic, cooperative, worker-run businesses, there is a sense that we are in life together. At Mondragon, not even the top-paid workers, the ones chosen to run the enterprise, can earn more than 6.5 times what the lowest-paid worker makes. In the United States, CEOs on average make 400 times the salary of the average worker in their corporation.

The more unequal a society, the more likely it is that life expectancy, children's educational performance, social mobility, and people's levels of trust will be lower—while rates of infant mortality, homicide, imprisonment, teenage births, mental illness, and alcohol and drug addiction will be higher.

Americans suffer from these blights more than any other wealthy developed nation in the world because we have the greatest inequality between our rich and poor people. The injuries are greatest for those on the bottom tiers, but inequality ultimately damages everyone.

Imagine knowing that we are all basically equal. No one would need to feel inferior or ashamed because she or he could not afford the lives of the rich and famous. Imagine if our media covered stories of regular working people as if we were special for our deeds, work, relationships, and lives.

Imagine eliminating capitalist profits from our health care. Imagine a nation that emphasizes preventative care to spare us illness. Imagine being taught a healthy lifestyle that could help to prevent obesity, heart disease, and diabetes. Imagine healthy food being promoted rather than junk food. Imagine family-style restaurants that have playgrounds and nutritious food and are as accessible and inexpensive as McDonald's is now. Imagine the cases of asthma plummeting because investing in lowering the level of environmental pollutants is understood to be efficient. Imagine the idea that it is efficient to produce health, so efficient that is worth the money to cut pollution.

Imagine getting care when we are sick without worrying about money. Imagine knowing that research on medications or medical devices was not funded by drug companies that will profit from the results but done by scientists with no financial stake in the outcome. Imagine our relief in knowing that the medications are effective and have no hidden or dangerous side effects. Imagine knowing that our caregivers were not constantly pushed to prescribe name-brand drugs and medical devices that produce corporate profits. Imagine knowing that our physician's primary interest is improving our health. Imagine our medical personnel taking lots of time to get to know us so they can better understand why we got sick.

Cuba is quite poor, and we are the richest large nation on earth. We spend more than 23 times as much per person for health care than they do, yet Cuba's infant mortality rate is lower than ours. We have the most costly medical system in the world. Imagine how healthy we could be in our rich nation if medicine were socialized like Cuba's.

The supports that hold us up as psychologically healthy humans are like a table. One leg of our mental health is intimate personal life with a partner, sometimes children, very close friends, and family members. A second leg is community, a wider circle of people who provide a set of deep connections around a shared interest or activity. That could be a sports team, a community project like a PTA, or a social-issue group working together on creating quality education, affordable day care, or clean air. Churches or political parties like the Green Party or movements like Occupy Wall Street can also provide that strong support in connecting around shared beliefs. A third leg of our mental health table is the sense of hope and security that comes from knowing we have opportunities to make a living and improve our lives. The fourth leg is the trust and friendship felt in egalitarian societies where people assume that we're all in this life together as equals.

All four legs of the American table of mental health are now wobbling. Americans are more and more socially isolated. Membership in such organized groups as the PTA and bowling leagues has dropped by more than half since 1970. Even more stunning, in a 2004 sociological survey, almost a quarter of the people interviewed said there was *no one* with whom they discussed "important matters," up from 10 percent in 1985. We have one of the highest divorce rates in the world. A majority of US marriages end in legal separation or divorce, and millions of unmarried couples split up without going through the legal system, leaving behind the pain of failure and loneliness for men, women, and especially children.

Hope for the future is hard to muster. According to US Department of Labor statistics from June 2012, people twenty to twenty-four years old have an official unemployment rate of 13.7 percent. Millions are underemployed, working part-time when they want full-time work or working in jobs far below their skill level. We have all met people like the young man with a master's degree in political science who is brewing and selling coffee at the local Starbucks. Many college graduates start their work lives loaded with debt. Imagine jobs and opportunities for all Americans.

Imagine giving families the kinds of support that make life and relationships at home less exhausting. Imagine lifting the weight of domestic work from the tired shoulders of American women. What could our lives be like if we, like many European nations, routinely provided quality free or heavily subsidized child care, after-school and summer care, child allowances, paid maternity leaves, paid guaranteed family leaves, and vacations? According to Human Rights Watch, 178 countries in the world have a legal guarantee of paid maternity leave; the three that don't are the United States, Papua New Guinea, and Swaziland. What could raising children be like if, as in Denmark or Estonia, we provided more than six months of paid leave for new parents? Even countries as poor as Bangladesh and Indonesia require employers to provide three months of paid parental leave. That would make our family lives much happier or, shall we say, more efficient in producing happiness.

What if *everyone* had some time to relax, not just wealthier Americans who can afford nanny care, maid service, meals out, drop-off laundry, and money for vacations. Imagine people coming home from work to rest, play with their kids, take a walk, or talk to one another. Imagine the real possibility that we could manage this with higher pay, shorter work hours, flexible family work schedules, and high-quality free child care.

Imagine a hopeful America.

For most adults, family and marriage are the basis of their emotional life. In divorce and separation, women usually suffer more economically, while men suffer more emotionally. Throughout their separations and divorces, women often retain close, emotionally sustaining bonds with other women and children, while men have a harder, lonelier time without their female partners. Is it efficient to have so few social and emotional supports that people without intimate partnerships regularly become isolated?

The logic of capitalist profit lowered people's wages. As soon as computers could replace humans and multinational communications systems allowed it, American jobs were outsourced to places where people work for lower wages and have few benefits. We did not have powerful socialist or communist unions to successfully fight outsourcing (as they do in most European nations). The crisis of lowered wages pushed American women into the labor force frequently out of necessity rather than by their own choice. Lowered wages altered the fabric of personal relationships so that personal support, emotional nurturance, and safety in the United States suffered. American women and families were not given the social supports that give men and women satisfying work outside of the home as well as time to enjoy their families.

Capitalism's reach stretches into the bedroom. Pornography is a multibillion-dollar industry; pornographic images and videos are widely accessible via the Internet. Millions of men and some women are purchasing solitary experiences even in sex, which is supposed to be about reciprocal connection; they are sitting alone with manufactured images that often contain degrading, racist, sexist, or violent messages about gender relationships and sexual intimacy. Capitalism values profit above all. Since such tunnel vision has no concern for equal rights or morality, how does the "efficient" mainstreaming of porn affect relationships?

Imagine a sexual life where people prefer the experience of intimate connection with an equal human being over profit-driven, degrading pornographic images. Imagine teaching children that sex is a mutually pleasurable connection. Here we might learn from social-democratic Sweden, which begins sex education in the first grade. It starts by teaching about how the flowers need to be pollinated to grow, continues through learning the intricate workings of the human body, and culminates in high school with talking about respect and caring for each other as well as any future children. Imagine the celebration of all kinds of mutual loving connections: gay, straight, and transgender.

Imagine a life without capitalist efficiency. Imagine stable jobs and time off for personal, social, and political activities and relationships. Imagine the empowerment of democracy at work.

Imagine high-quality universal child care, health care, and education, including sex education and education in relationship-building.

Of course we can afford it. Imagine using the vast funds paid out in corporate subsidies to care for our families and sustain our personal happiness. Imagine how the more than $1 trillion spent on the wars in Iraq and Afghanistan could be used instead to create jobs that give us the time and benefits to nurture one another and our children. Imagine a sturdy table of personal, community, and social support among equals.

Chapter 9

A Woman's Workday in a Socialist USA

Renate Bridenthal

Imagine waking up looking forward to going to work. You think about your plans even while having breakfast.

Imagine meeting up with a team of people with whom you're working on a project: to make something, design something, deliver a special kind of service.

Imagine the meeting. Your teammates have arrived with new ideas, too, and you bat around those ideas all morning until a solid plan emerges.

Imagine dividing up the work to be done, each teammate volunteering his or her best skill, without barriers of gender or race.

Imagine breaking for an hour's lunch at a restaurant in or near your workplace that serves a selection of good, healthy foods at a reasonable price.

Imagine an afternoon putting your morning's plan into action, focused on your own piece of the project, knowing that others are focusing on theirs. In the hour before the day's work is done, there is another meeting to discuss what has been accomplished and what remains to be done to complete the project.

Imagine that after the project is done, your team—or a group of teams in your company—meets to discuss how your product is to be sold or implemented. You have a voice in that final decision. There is no boss. The teams own the company.

Imagine that, best of all, you have an equal share in the profit earned by that product or service. The teams will decide how much money to reinvest in the company to ensure its continuing success and how much to divide among yourselves. As a woman, you will bring home as fairly earned an income as your partner, if you have one, which means your home relationship will not be soured by financial inequality.

Which brings us to the issue of work and family, something that has exhausted women in particular through the ages up to and including yesterday. With all the new labor-saving technology, a shortened workweek of, say, twenty-five hours, frees up time for personal and family affairs. And even these hours can be organized flexibly, a concept developed in the late twentieth century that lets workers choose their schedules within agreed limits. Such an arrangement could result in a workweek of variable hours, depending on the needs of your workplace and your personal requirements, a complex formula that future data processing will be able to establish.

On your way home, you may pick up your child or children (if your partner has not already done so) from kindergarten or an after-school program, where they have enjoyed a rich social and educational experience led by childcare professionals.

Imagine that having children while holding a job is no problem. You could choose to stay home to take care of your new baby—you'll get your full pay, and your job will be held for your return. You could also return to work as soon as possible, because you like your job and your teammates, and you want to continue in your career. Imagine bringing your baby along to the workplace nursery, where you can go to breast-feed at intervals, where she or he will otherwise be cared for by trained professionals.

Imagine that, having returned home from work, you can choose to make dinner with your partner or to eat in the dining room of your communally owned living space. Afterward, you might enjoy a leisurely evening at home; take in a movie, a play, or a concert; play games in the entertainment room of your commune; or go out for a walk while a caregiver, whom you pay or with whom you trade services, babysits for a few hours. You might also choose to take some classes to upgrade your skills or explore something new.

Imagine that after a full night's sleep, you awake fresh and excited about a new day, looking forward to the shared work with your colleagues.

Chapter 10

Dignity, Respect, Equality, Love

Blanche Wiesen Cook

As we imagine a future defined by justice, economic democracy, and political freedom, our path is illuminated by many women who envisioned an end to poverty and dedicated their lives to movements for human betterment and global peace. Many of these women left lasting legacies that allow us to continue the struggle for respect across all our racial, religious, and ethnic differences.

Jane Addams (1860–1935), Lillian D. Wald (1867–1940), and Crystal Eastman (1881–1928) were three of them. They were community builders whose words have galvanized generations of activists. Appalled by the poverty and neglect they witnessed at home and in their travels, and motivated by love for and a sense of responsibility to people who suffered, Addams and Wald became America's most progressive social workers.

In 1889, Addams opened Hull House, a community center in Chicago. It provided health care, education, and English classes for newly arrived immigrants; counseling for families and workers, including meetings with trade unionists to oppose child labor and discrimination; recreation and cultural activities; and classes in art, music, and poetry. Wald, trained as a nurse, opened the Henry Street Settlement House in New York in 1893. It provided similar services, emphasizing health care, and included the Neighborhood Playhouse theater. She also launched the Visiting Home Nurse Service, with first-aid stations, nurse education programs, and convalescent centers throughout the city. In 1912, she was elected the first president of the National Organization for Public Health.

Addams and Wald shared a commitment to international peace and women's suffrage and empowerment with radical journalist Crystal Eastman. Eastman, dramatic and determined, was an orator and athlete. Her vision of women's power included "women's right to physical equality with men." She imagined a female utopia of athletes where women would be "unhampered by preconceived ideas of what was fit or proper or possible."

"When women were expected to be agile, they became agile," she proclaimed. "When they were expected to be brave, they developed courage; when they had to endure, their endurance broke all records."

In 1907, Eastman graduated second in her class at New York University Law School and embarked on her legal career as a labor investigator. In 1910, her report "Work Accidents and the Law" detailed the cruel conditions and appalling neglect American workers suffered. It generated a new movement for workers' rights and occupational health and safety. She served on the US Commission for Industrial Relations, drafted New York State's first workers' compensation law (the model for the nation), and became a dedicated socialist and feminist activist. In 1911, after the Triangle Shirtwaist Factory fire in New York City killed 146 people, mostly young women, she wrote that when healthy women and men die of preventable disasters, we do not want to discuss relief funds, "we want to start a revolution."

Convinced that women's empowerment was the first step toward that revolution, she cofounded, with Alice Paul and other equal-rights feminists, the Congressional Union for Woman Suffrage in 1913. That year, she was also a delegate to the International Woman Suffrage Congress in Budapest, Hungary.

Addams, Wald, and Eastman worked closely together to end World War I, to keep the United States neutral, and to fight US imperialism in Latin America and the Caribbean. They lobbied, protested, and wrote numerous articles as they sought to imagine and build a society where wars would be impossible. They launched the American Union Against Militarism, which spawned the American Civil Liberties Union to defend democracy—freedom of speech, press, assembly "and freedom of conscience—the essentials of liberty. . . . To maintain something over here that will be worth coming back to when the weary war is over." They also founded the Woman's Peace Party, which became the Women's International League for Peace and Freedom (WILPF).

After the war, Eastman became convinced that the only way to restore liberty was to achieve socialism. In WILPF's journal, *Four Lights*, she hailed the Russian Revolution "with mad, glad joy." In a December 1920 article, "Now We Can Begin," she wrote that many feminists were socialists or communists who knew "that the vast majority of women as well as men are without property . . . bread-and-butter slaves under a system of society which allows the very sources of life to be privately owned by a few" and counted themselves part of "the working-class army that is marching to overthrow that system."

But real change, Eastman believed, also required a women's revolution. Women's slavery did not come from the profit system alone, and their emancipation would not be ensured by its downfall. Too many "revolutionary" men, she wrote, disregarded women's needs: "'My wife is all right,' he says. And his wife, one usually finds, is raising his children in a Bronx flat or a dreary suburb, to which he returns occasionally for food and sleep when all possible excitement . . . has been wrung" from the day.

For socialism to embrace all humanity, women had to have equal opportunity "to exercise their infinitely varied gifts in infinitely varied ways, instead of being destined . . . [to] housework and child-raising." Should women choose housework and child-raising as an occupation, she said, it should be "recognized by the world as work," and paid a just wage.

Eastman demanded equal pay for equal work and a "revolution in the early training and education of both boys and girls. It must be womanly as well as manly to earn your own living, to stand on your own feet. And it must be manly as well as womanly to know how to cook and sew and clean and take care of yourself." She was aware that "men will not give up their privilege of helplessness without a struggle" and that they actually "cultivated ignorance about household matters."

Impressed that many of her friends and allies, including Jane Addams and Lillian Wald, lived communally with their best beloveds in their settlement houses and summer residences, Eastman noted that two women could "'make a home' together without either one being overburdened or over-bored. It is because they both know how and both feel responsible." They create "a pleasant partnership, more fun than work." But when a man and woman live together, "it is almost never a partnership—the woman simply adds running the home to her regular outside job. Unless she is very strong, it is too much for her, she gets tired and bitter."

The solution was socialism and feminism, women's empowerment that involved sexual freedom, voluntary motherhood, and choices about love and lust. "Feminists are not nuns," Eastman wrote in an article about birth control. "We want to be loved, and most of us want children. . . . But we want our love to be joyous and free." That freedom would require political and economic equality between women and men. To that end, in 1923, she was one of four members of Alice Paul's Woman's Party who drafted and campaigned for an Equal Rights Amendment to the Constitution. This, she said, was the most important "fight worth fighting, even if it takes ten years." (Congress approved the ERA in 1972, but only thirty-five states ratified it. The struggle to pass it continues.)

America's post–World War I "red scare" derailed efforts toward socialism and feminism until the Depression. Eastman lived mostly in England until her death in 1928. Jane Addams was awarded a Nobel Peace Prize in 1931 but was nonetheless attacked as "the most dangerous woman in America" in 1935, the year of her death. Brazilian Catholic Archbishop Dom Hélder Câmara, one of the founders of liberation theology, which was later condemned by the Vatican, said years later, "When I feed the poor, they call me a saint. When I ask why the poor have no food, they call me a communist," a quote that became a popular poster.

Increasingly, however, progressive and socialist women understood that economic security combined with feminism and sexual freedom were required for individual serenity and community harmony. While Crystal Eastman never believed male-dominated socialist parties could be counted on to fulfill that promise, the Russian feminist Alexandra Kollontai (1872–1952) believed that women's liberation required socialism.

Kollontai was born Alexandra Mikhailovna Domontovich in St. Petersburg, the daughter of a tsarist general and an affluent Finnish-born mother, both of the old Russian nobility. She grew up in the countryside, where she witnessed "the injustice of adults." She was "particularly and painfully shocked" that everything had been given to her, "whereas so much was denied to the other children," the peasant children who were her playmates.

She was determined to be free to live her life according to her own needs and wants. At eighteen, against her parents' wishes, she married her cousin Vladimir Kollontai, "an impecunious young engineer." But her domestic "happiness lasted hardly three years," and in 1898 she left her husband and son to study political economy at the University of Zurich. From then on, she devoted her life to women's freedom and equality. In 1908, her book *Finland and Socialism* resulted in a warrant for her arrest. She left for England and toured Germany, Canada, and the United States, and then moved to Paris, where she was close to socialists Rosa Luxemburg, Clara Zetkin, and Bertrand and Dora Russell.

Kollontai lectured widely and inspired countless women and men dedicated to human betterment. When Russian journalist Ilya Ehrenburg first heard her lecture in Paris in 1909, he was deeply moved by her observation that "personal happiness, for which we were created, was unthinkable without universal happiness."

She remained in exile until 1917. After the Russian Revolution in October 1917, the Communist Party's Central Committee created a women's department, the Zhenotdel, to wage a widespread literacy and women's rights campaign. Kollontai was appointed people's commissar for social welfare. She organized homes for maternity and infant care, drafted decrees on the care of mother and child, issued health and nutritional standards, legalized birth control, and wrote the first Soviet marriage and divorce laws, which were characterized by equality.

In 1919, she introduced her more expansive vision of the "New Woman" in a workers' democracy. Supported by new ideas of reproductive rights and communal family arrangements, the New Woman—educated, economically independent, sexually liberated—would flourish. Women's servitude to the family, state, and society would be replaced by equality, shared learning, and freedom for all physical and emotional experiences. Unpossessed, she would have no interest in possession. She would be free to fulfill herself and her own needs to work and be creative.

"The woman of the past had been raised to adopt a negligent attitude toward herself," Kollontai wrote. "But now every woman was free to fulfill her needs, exercise her profession, work in service to ideas and community, create healthy, joyous sexual relations. History has never seen such variety of personal relationships." Socialism required "a basic transformation of the human psyche" that enabled people to "achieve relationships based on the unfamiliar ideas of complete freedom, equality, genuine friendship."

In 1923, Kollontai published her most controversial article, "Make Way for Winged Eros," to celebrate "multifaceted love." Socialism's task, she wrote, was not to drive away Eros, but to create informed sexual "relationships in the spirit of the great new psychological force of comradely solidarity," which embraced a new respect for different love relationships among society's many differing people—all free to choose. Her vision was initially supported by Dr. Grigorii Batkis, director of the Moscow Institute of Social Hygiene, who affirmed Russia's "sexual revolution," which meant "the absolute non-interference of the state and society in sexual matters, so long as nobody is injured." It also affirmed homosexual rights and decreed that all forms of "sexual gratification are natural, and all forms of sexual intercourse are private matters."

But Communist Party opposition to Kollontai's views intensified. Between 1925 and 1927, a wave of terror and brutality confronted Muslim women in Zhenodtel clubs in the Crimea and throughout the Soviet east. In 1929, Joseph Stalin halted the modernization campaign and disbanded the women's commission. After 1922, Kollontai lived abroad, mostly as Soviet ambassador to Norway, Mexico, and, from 1930–1946, Sweden. Although she survived Stalin's tyranny, repression, and purges, partly because of her international influence, her views were discarded in Russia. She died in 1952 in Moscow, surrounded mostly by feminist friends and colleagues.

During the last months of her life, she pondered her exile, possible new beginnings, and imagined the future: "The world never stagnates, it is always stirring, new forms of life are always appearing." She looked forward to a wonderful future of "Happiness. Happiness for everyone."

Despite America's several red scares and the Soviet state's turn to repression, the words of these twentieth-century visionaries have endured and continue to move us forward. Activist women read Kollontai around the world. Jane Addams and Lillian Wald influenced Eleanor Roosevelt (1884–1962), who began her adult life teaching calisthenics and dance at a New York settlement house.

Eleanor Roosevelt fought for women's rights, civil rights, and human rights throughout her life, convinced that to end war, we must end poverty. As first lady from 1933 to 1945, she urged her husband, Franklin Delano Roosevelt, to extend Social Security to all Americans and to include in the program health and housing security—two items still on the American legislative agenda. The agonies of World War II intensified her conviction that a peaceful future depended on a New Deal for all the world's people. She repeatedly spoke out against discrimination, segregation, poverty, and greed. She believed the United Nations, which issued its Universal Declaration of Human Rights in 1948, would lead the world toward racial harmony and "a spirit of mutual responsibility for human welfare."

During the 1970s, a second wave of feminism rediscovered the legacy of these and many other socialist women. Two who especially inspired me were my friends and mentors Dorothy

Healy and Annette Rubenstein. Healy, an activist, journalist, and radio broadcaster who lived a fighting life, said to me one day, "I don't get ulcers. I never get ulcers. I give ulcers." Rubenstein, a scholar, activist, and editor, frequently said, "We will have socialism, or we will have barbarism."

Today, with war and poverty epidemic and an intensified assault against women and women's rights, it is time. Imagine Code Pink and Pussy Riot worldwide. Imagine Socialism.

Chapter 11

How Queer Life Might Be Different in a Socialist USA

Leslie Cagan and Melanie Kaye/Kantrowitz

When a handful of gay men and transvestites fought back against yet one more police raid on a gay bar in New York in June 1969, no one could have imagined what was being unleashed. It didn't take long for gays, lesbians, and other nonconforming sexual minorities to find the power of a collective, public voice. Within months a new movement was in the streets, a movement that added a new layer of insight into the complexity of human behavior and the ways social, cultural, political, and economic structures define our lives.

At this moment in history, we are asking how our lives as lesbians, gay men, bisexuals, transgender people, and those questioning and exploring their sexuality (LGBTQ) might be different in the context of socialism. Today, it's a little hard to see how this might happen, how massive numbers of people would move our nation from capitalism to socialism in a nonviolent revolution. But because we know how capitalism undermines our humanity and corrupts human interaction, we believe it is inevitable that this malignant economic system will collapse and be replaced by what we call socialism.

Our concept of socialism is not limited to restructuring work and economic activity. It embraces altering the full range of social, cultural, political, and familial structures and power relations. It goes far beyond just having an economic structure that's grounded in meeting our collective needs instead of one based on private profit. We cannot imagine creating socialism without eradicating racism, for instance. Our analysis and organizing practice must understand how different kinds of oppressive power relations—those based in race, gender, and sexuality, as well as in economic activity—are interwoven and give shape to one another. Just as our lives are not merely the work we do, the socialism we build must address all aspects of power, all of the institutional forces that affect our lives.

Our experience as workers is not merely shaped by the wage we earn or the power the boss has over us. For example, a black, Latina, or other woman of color is much more likely to be paid less and treated worse by her bosses than a straight white man. Our personal experiences of capitalism are informed by how we experience race, gender, and sexuality. And this cuts all ways: how we experience race is informed by our class, gender, and sexuality realities, and so forth.

The socialism we envision will build on the strengths and insights of what's often referred to as identity politics, while avoiding its pitfalls and weaknesses. The movements of people of color, women, LGBTQ people, youth, seniors, the disabled, and more all uncovered layers of oppression and shed new light on the dynamics and hierarchies of power. Only by weaving together the movements that attack abusive power in all of its manifestations will we be strong enough to tackle the monster of capitalism.

What will queer people's lives be like after we've displaced capitalism and built a new socialism? We can start with the basics: an end to discrimination, bigotry, and hatred. Each of us accepted for the fullness of who and what we are, including our sexual and gender identities. No one turned away from a job or denied a promotion because of their queerness. No one barred from housing because of their family relations. No one mocked or bullied or harassed because of their sexuality or the perception of their sexuality. No killing, no violence.

LGBTQ people would have the same access as straight people to all cultural, social, political, and economic structures and would be part of reshaping those structures. For instance, if marriage is still needed to help ensure the rights of loving couples, then all LGBTQ people who wanted to would be able to marry. LGBTQ people would be able to have, or adopt, and raise children either as single parents, with a partner, or within a more complex family structure.

All of that is just the first layer, just the starting point. The LGBTQ struggle has shed light on issues that people have dealt with from the beginning of time—issues of sexuality and sexual expression, gender and gender identity. But shedding light does not necessarily mean finding all of the answers. In fact, perhaps some questions have no definitive answer. Are our sexual desires and needs determined by biology—are we born this way? Or do we make choices and have conscious preferences? Or might there be some combination of these forces at play?

Living in a socialist society would not mean that all these issues will be settled; it would mean that all of the hard questions would be out in the open for full discussion because we'd be living in a culture that encouraged honest exploration of every aspect of our lives. All of the possibilities of love, sexual expression, and gender identity would be accepted as part of the human experience. (This does not mean that each individual would have to engage in all variations of those.) There would be no compulsory monogamy, and no campaigns to "smash monogamy." There would be no obligation to marry, just as there would be no restrictions on marriage. Indeed, the whole notion of marriage might shift since there would be no special privileges associated with it.

No one would be denied the right to explore their own sexual and gender realities, needs, and desires. There would be no shame assigned to sexual desires. In fact, desire would be appreciated for the role it plays in helping to make us full human beings. Sex would not be defined as primarily or solely an activity to ensure the survival of the human race, but as the pleasurable, joyful, desire-filling interaction between people it can be. It would be appreciated and encouraged, while no one would be forced into sexual activity. The layers of embarrassment that are all too often now associated with sex would be stripped away. And in that process, the positive power of sexuality would be released and honored.

The creation of socialism would allow for a new exploration of sexuality. There will still be many questions people answer differently, such as issues of monogamy or polyamory, challenges communities will struggle with, and concerns to which we might not always find common approaches.

Even complex and sometimes troubling issues such as sex between adults and minors would be discussed without assumptions of guilt or imposition of shame. For instance, would there be an "age of consent" that most people are comfortable with, and if so, what might that be? A relationship between a boy of sixteen or seventeen who is just coming out and a gay man in his thirties or forties might be quite positive and healthy, but it might still bother some people. And unless sexism and racism have been eradicated, how would racial or male/female power dynamics factor into these issues?

Also, where would lines be drawn: Is there not a difference between a sixteen-year-old and a ten-year-old, for example? Are lines to be drawn when it comes to sadism or masochism, desires related to submission and domination, or bondage and discipline? If there are such lines, a major concern would be how issues of enforcement might play out.

In a socialist culture, the current norms of male and female gender identity would be things of the past. Gender identity would not be based on the biological differences between male and female, although we certainly would not hide or deny those differences. People would not be mocked for what they were, or how they walk down the street. How we dressed our bodies would be based entirely on our own choices. Each of us would be encouraged to love and respect our own bodies and, therefore, the bodies of other people. At the same time, the decision to alter one's body or to change one's gender would also be respected and accepted.

Sex would not be a commodity to be bought and sold on the market. Capitalism makes everything a commodity—soon we will be charged for the air we breathe! In socialism, things will probably still be bought and sold, but the decisions about what to make and what to sell, about how to make things and how to sell them, will be based on what people need and not on what increases the coffers of individuals or expands the power of privately owned enterprises.

The women's liberation movement shed light on the ways women's bodies have been used as promotional tools to sell a wide range of products. Of course, women's bodies (and also those of children and men) have for centuries been sold or rented for the pleasure of (mostly) men. This would come to an end under socialism. Or would it? This is another one of those hard questions.

We are not critical of sex workers, and we know there are many reasons people have taken up this line of work, not necessarily just economic need. We can imagine that there might still be some type of sex workers within a socialist culture, but just as all other types of work relations will be different than what we experience under capitalism, we would hope that their work relations would not be based on exploitation, abuse of power, and fear of violence.

Under socialism, LGBTQ people will have the full civil, legal, and human rights that everyone will benefit from. Beyond that, because the insights of both the feminist and the queer liberation movements will have been absorbed into the core analysis and philosophy of the struggle for socialism, everyone will be able to more fully experience who they are, how they express themselves sexually, and their own gender identity.

All of this will be integrated into the new realities that our work against racism, sexism, and the oppression and exploitation of capitalist class relations will have brought to the creation of socialism. None of these pieces will find fruition without the other parts being in full force. Our vision of socialism brings it all together, for the benefit of all.

Chapter 12

Drugs in a Society Where People Care About Each Other

Steven Wishnia

Getting intoxicated is an indelible part of human life, from kava in Vanuatu to cabernet in Paris. It's one of the great pleasures of life for millions of people. But the results are often unhealthy for both individuals and society as a whole.

For the past half century, the world's main answer to this problem has been prohibiting all drugs except for alcohol and defining all use of illegal drugs as "abuse." Yet prohibition has never created the drug-free society its supporters tout. In the United States, it has fed organized crime networks all over the globe and led to the incarceration of hundreds of thousands of people—more than 90 percent of them black or Latino in some states.

So how can we manage this problem according to the principles of economic and social justice? How can we balance individuals' freedom to alter their brain chemistry in pleasurable ways with the common good of not having people drive while impaired or be too wasted to function?

Marijuana, by far the most widely used illegal drug, would be the easiest to legalize. Production, sales, and consumption could be managed under a system similar to that already used for alcohol. This would involve age limits for buying it, a ban on driving while intoxicated, and regulations on distribution, sales, and public use. Taxes on it would finance this regulatory system, with any surplus going to drug education, treatment, and the general welfare. We would also save both the money spent on enforcing the current laws and the social costs of illegal business and arresting more than 800,000 people a year.

One obvious model is the Dutch "coffee shop" system. In the Netherlands, especially in Amsterdam, cannabis coffee shops operate openly, like a combination of bars and liquor stores. Any adult can go in and buy up to five grams, either to smoke on the premises or take home. Growing marijuana remains illegal, though, so Dutch authorities usually ignore the supply sources in order to preserve the system. (In 2011, the country's right-wing government enacted a law restricting the coffee shops to Dutch residents. Amsterdam resisted that law, but it went into effect in May 2012 in the provinces along the Belgian and German borders. Within a month, the small border city of Maastricht had received more than six hundred complaints about street dealers.)

As the United States already has thousands of marijuana growers, home cultivation would have to be a part of any legalization system. If marijuana were grown on small farms (no Philip Morris–type plantations), it would be a vital source of income for rural areas, and consumers would enjoy the fruits of these growers' well-developed expertise.

Legal marijuana would also reduce the environmental damage caused by illicit cultivation. The twin threats of arrest and theft have forced many growers indoors, where they use massive amounts of electricity. Clandestine outdoor growers often farm wilderness areas, where they exploit the water supply and pollute it with fertilizer runoff. In addition, hemp, the variety of cannabis cultivated for fiber instead of THC, would be very useful for paper, cloth, and construction materials (although probably not as much as some marijuana evangelists claim).

One obstacle to marijuana legalization is that there is no definitive test to determine whether someone is too high to drive. On the other hand, this would be less of an issue in a society with adequate public transportation. (In the United States today, alcohol is part of most social activity, and in most places driving is the only way to get around.)

Legalization would also separate the medical marijuana system from the recreational market. Therapeutic cannabis could be handled like a more sophisticated form of herbal medicine, under better medical supervision than is now possible in the states where it is semi-legal.

A legal marijuana industry could also provide thousands of union jobs, from gardeners to "budtenders," says Dan Rush, California organizing director for the United Food and Commercial Workers. The UFCW is organizing workers in the state's medical-cannabis dispensaries and campaigned for Proposition 19, the 2010 ballot initiative that would have legalized the sale and cultivation of pot in California. These jobs would pay as much as $35 an hour, Rush says.

Other drugs present much more complicated issues. Although patterns of use vary among individuals, heroin, cocaine, and amphetamine users are much more likely to develop serious problems. Therefore, it probably wouldn't be good to make those drugs as easily accessible as alcohol or cannabis. "As the drugs become more dangerous, the regulations would be stricter," says Jack Cole of Law Enforcement Against Prohibition.

The guiding principle here should be what is called "harm reduction." Its basic precept is that people are going to do drugs anyway, so their use should be channeled toward ways that do the least harm as much as possible. For example, if people are going to get drunk, they shouldn't drive. If people are going to do heroin, it's better that they finance it by working instead of by theft or prostitution.

The needle-exchange programs that emerged in the early 1990s in response to the AIDS crisis are the primary example of harm reduction. Their principle is that giving people clean needles to shoot heroin and other drugs is less socially harmful than users contracting and spreading HIV by sharing dirty needles.

Heroin maintenance for addicts is one possible solution. Programs in Switzerland and Britain have shown promising signs that this stabilizes addicts' lives, reduces crime and the transmission of HIV, and undercuts the illegal market by taking away its most regular customers.

Switzerland began heroin maintenance in 1994 after a disastrous experiment with tolerating open use in one park in Zurich. The government opened clinics where confirmed addicts could get as much pharmaceutical-quality heroin as they wanted for about $10 a day, as long as they used it only on the premises. The results were that crime dropped, more addicts got jobs, and much of the illegal market dried up, as occasional users didn't buy enough to support it.

The United Kingdom has let doctors prescribe heroin to addicts since the 1920s, but the practice has been curtailed sharply since the late 1960s. "It was only when the program stopped that you began to have a drug problem in the UK," the Rolling Stones' Keith Richards wrote in his autobiography. Still, he called the program "a beautiful scam," as registered addicts could easily get more than they needed and sell the rest.

However, people who want to get high will always seek out substitutes. In the United States, heroin use seems to have declined over the last decade, but use of prescription opioids, such as OxyContin, Vicodin, and Percocet, has mushroomed, especially in rural areas where heroin is not as readily available. These are also addictive, but at least users get purer drugs and a fixed dose.

Regulating cocaine and other stimulant drugs is much more problematic. A single approach won't work because the range of individual use is extreme. Someone snorting a few lines of coke once a month will do far less damage than a crackhead breaking into cars to keep a five-day binge going. Also, maintenance would not be a practical solution, as cocaine and amphetamine abuse often involves binging, not steady-dose addiction. Therefore, any form of harm reduction has to be social and psychological, which is to say subjective and imperfect.

This brings up one of the main problems in dealing with drug abuse. Even if rehab were easily available, not everyone would want to go. Some antisocial behavior is inevitable. There are no panaceas, and there will always be people with problems. We are dealing with an anarchic, Dionysiac side of human psychology. We can't eliminate it, but we can try to direct it away from destructive behavior. That means that the people conceiving and running a harm-reduction system must be pragmatic, not dogmatic, and willing to experiment with different approaches. "I am certain that I don't know what model will work," says Eric Sterling of the Criminal Justice Policy Foundation. "I don't have the answer, and I don't know anybody who does. It would be nice if all of these were neat, soluble packages. Unfortunately, they're not."

"Educate, educate, educate," urges Joyce Rivera, director of St. Ann's Harm Reduction Corner in New York's South Bronx. Current US drug education is the spawn of Reagan-era drug hysteria, almost as full of mythology and scare tactics as abstinence-only sex education. Its lies—for example, that marijuana is the equivalent of heroin—destroy the credibility of its truths.

Better drug education would inform people of what the effects and dangers of different drugs are, and stress "set and setting," the emotional and psychological expectations people bring to drugs and the environment in which they use them. It would also teach people how to recognize addictive or destructive patterns of use.

Set and setting are particularly important for MDMA (Exstasy) and the psychedelics. These have the least addictive potential of any class of drugs, but they can exacerbate psychiatric problems. A legal distribution system might involve a combination of risk waiver, education, and a check for psychiatric symptoms.

If drugs were more easily available, the social problems they might produce must be measured against the harm done by prohibition—crime caused by high prices and disputes within the illegal market, corruption, overdose deaths and disease exacerbated by furtive use, and forcing users into a way-of-life subculture that isolates them from society.

Alcohol, the most widely used drug in the world, is one of the most destructive. It exacts a fearsome toll in disease, car accidents, and drunken violence. Yet the main accomplishments of the US government's attempt to outlaw it were giving crime networks a lucrative source of income and poisoning hundreds of drinkers with dubious booze. Ironically, the 1919–1933 Prohibition laws would be considered "decriminalization" today, as possessing alcohol remained legal.

Prohibition pushes the market toward stronger forms of drugs, as they are more concealable and profitable. Legalization would likely move people toward milder forms; the Dutch tolerance of cannabis coffee shops was conceived to separate marijuana users from the market for harder drugs. This wouldn't work in all cases; those who freebase cocaine might not be satisfied with chewing coca leaves. On the other hand, beer is far more popular than 151-proof rum.

Societies have also developed cultural ways to reduce alcohol problems, from designated drivers to bartenders and friends cutting drunks off. Though you can buy a lethal dose of alcohol in any liquor store, we don't have a nation of alcoholics. Few people are completely abstinent, but most adults can handle their drinking and drug use. The problems come from those who, for emotional or possibly genetic reasons, can't or won't control theirs, and from those who have not yet learned their limits.

Ultimately, preventing self-destructive drug use is a social and spiritual question. People who are happy still drink and get high, but they are far less likely to have problems with it than people who do not feel like part of a community, who were abused as children, who feel they have no future.

The Soviet Union was a dismal, vodka-soaked place to live, but after the fall of communism in 1991, Russia and former Soviet republics such as Belarus and Ukraine became the only region of the world outside the AIDS belt of southern Africa where life expectancy actually dropped. Overnight, these societies turned into kleptocracies with extreme economic inequality, where gangsters became multimillionaires and working people were lucky if they could afford a loaf of bread. Their death rate jumped, fed by cirrhosis, other alcohol-related diseases, and the highest rates of HIV infection in Europe, fueled by needle drug use.

Those are all signs of a society without hope. Hope is in short supply in the ruthless plutocracy our nation has become.

It may be naïve and nebulous to say this, but in the long run, the best way to keep drug use from becoming drug abuse is to create a society where people care about each other, where they feel like they're part of a community, where they feel like they're worth more than their mere market value.

Chapter 13

Immigration: Immigrant Workers Point the Way to a Better World

Juan Gonzalez

Between March and May of 2006, an estimated 3 to 5 million people, most of them Latinos, filled the downtown streets of some 160 American towns and cities in the largest series of mass protests the nation had ever seen.

Not even during the heyday of the American labor movement in the 1930s or the high tide of civil rights protests and public opposition to the Vietnam War during the 1960s had such astonishing numbers paraded peacefully in so many different localities to express a common grievance. Never before had a group at the margins of US society taken our political establishment by such complete surprise. Word of the mobilizations, it turned out, had spread largely via Spanish-language radio and TV and through social networks of young Latinos on the Internet, so government leaders and the general public had little idea of what was happening until the huge crowds suddenly started to appear on our city streets.

The marchers' immediate goal was to defeat a bill in Congress (known as the Sensenbrenner bill, after its House sponsor,

Wisconsin Republican James Sensenbrenner) that would have established tough new penalties for immigrants who were in the country illegally. They sought not only to derail that legislation but also to replace it with a comprehensive overhaul of US immigration policy, one that would include a "path to citizenship" for an estimated twelve million undocumented workers already in the country. Protest leaders framed their efforts as a moral call for compassion and respect, for *dignidad* for illegal immigrants. Many adopted the slogan "*¡Si se puede!*" ("yes we can"), the nearly forgotten words that legendary Mexican American labor organizer Cesar Chavez had coined some forty years earlier for his United Farm Workers Organizing Committee.

Their message reverberated from the bustling streets of established Latino neighborhoods in the major cities to scores of new *barrios* that had sprung up in small towns and hamlets across the American heartland. The rallies they scheduled swelled with tens of thousands of maids, nannies, and maintenance workers, with lowly gardeners and day laborers, with restaurant busboys and dishwashers, with hotel waiters and bellhops, with hardened slaughterhouse workers and construction hardhats, many of whom had quietly led a furtive existence in the shadows of society, always afraid of being stopped by a local cop or sheriff or of being caught in an immigration raid and hastily deported. Suddenly, this brown-skinned and once-docile mass of humanity was parading through glistening city centers in broad daylight. With spouses and children at their sides and their infants in strollers, they proudly marched with their entire Pentecostal or Catholic congregations, their ministers and church banners at the front, waving both the American flag and those of their native countries.

These were not simply gatherings of the undocumented, however. Hundreds of thousands of Latinos who had been born in the United States or become naturalized citizens, or who were longtime legal residents, also participated. And leading the way in virtually every protest were startling numbers of US-born Hispanic high school and college students, many of them facing the prospect of their immigrant parents of being deported and being separated from them.

All shared the same burning sense of outrage. All were fed up with the mainstream media's reigning stereotype that depicts hordes of Latinos and undocumented workers as a new menace engulfing the country.

Although Latinos made up the overwhelming number of marchers, they were hardly alone; joining them as well were thousands of Polish, Irish, Korean, Chinese, and Filipino immigrants, along with many white and black religious and labor leaders and supporters.

The immigration protests of 2006 marked a rare example of an outcast group suddenly rising up and forcing the majority to rethink accepted notions of democratic and human rights. For most of the marchers, it was their first act of social protest, one that would permanently alter the way they viewed the world. For just as the 1963 March on Washington defined the outlook of many black Americans, and just as the college rebellions of 1968 shaped the thinking of a generation of white Americans, so too did these protests represent a political coming of age for the nation's Hispanic minority.

The new movement failed to achieve its main goal of immigration-law reform, yet it still left a deep and unexpected imprint on the entire country, for its stunning rise effectively marked the end of thirty years of conservative domination over national politics. Six months after the immigration protests, Democrats won control of both houses of Congress for the first time since 1994, and one of the chief reasons for that historic power shift was the mushrooming Latino vote. The number of Hispanics casting ballots that November jumped by nearly one million over the previous midterm election, from 4.7 million in 2002 to 5.6 million in 2006. And since the Republican Party was most closely associated with the Sensenbrenner bill, the percentage of Latinos who cast ballots for Republican candidates for the House of Representatives plummeted from 38 percent to 30 percent.

Then in 2008, Illinois Democratic Senator Barack Obama, borrowing the "Yes we can" slogan of Chavez's United Farm Workers and the immigrant-rights movement, captured the White House. Obama owed his historic victory in no small measure to the overwhelming support he received from Latino voters. Some 9.7 million Hispanics cast ballots for president in 2008, 2.1 million more than in 2004. Obama garnered 67 percent of those votes, while Republican John McCain received just 31 percent, with McCain's share representing a significant drop from the 40 percent Latino support George W. Bush enjoyed in the 2004 election.

The 2.1 million additional Latino voters in 2008 mirrored a similar jump among African Americans. Along with a sharp increase of more than 300,000 Asian Americans, it produced the most diverse electorate in the nation's history and ensured the election of our first black president. In the euphoric aftermath of Obama's election, many claimed the United States had entered a new, post-racial era.

A dispassionate view of voting statistics, however, did not provide such comforting visions of change, nor did the rise of the right-wing Tea Party movement soon after. Obama, after all, had received the support of only 43 percent of white voters, while John McCain amassed 55 percent. Such a yawning gap among whites would normally signal a Republican victory. Only the enormous turnout and overwhelming support Obama generated among the country's racial minorities—95 percent of African Americans voted for him, as did 62 percent of Asian

Americans—made it possible for him to win the election handily. His success thus reflected more about how the country's electorate was changing than it did about whether his policies represented a new direction.

When I began writing about immigration, at the end of the 1990s, the federal government was in the early stages of erecting a wall between Mexico and the United States, just south of San Diego. The makeshift barrier, I noted then, was not nearly as impressive as our planet's great testament to human insecurity, the 1,500-mile-long Great Wall that China's emperors spent centuries building against the Huns. Nonetheless, the American version was a clear indication that the US-Mexico border had become the epicenter of momentous changes in our hemisphere. By day, a constant stream of trucks headed south, carrying goods to newly erected factories bustling with nearly a million low-wage workers; by night, a silent flood of people headed north in search of the US wages that could spell survival for family members the migrants had left behind. Both movements were creating huge windfalls for tiny investor elites on both sides of the border, while furthering horrendous social conditions on the Mexican side.

We have not yet fully understood how massive immigration to the United States is the unintended human harvest of the nation's empire-building. Most of us rarely think of this country as an empire, even if Wall Street's currency speculators and investment bankers have repeatedly demonstrated their ability to wreck entire economies halfway around the globe in a matter of hours—a power far greater than the Roman or Ottoman rulers ever wielded. But during the last half of the twentieth century, and especially after the collapse of the Soviet Union, American corporations, backed wholeheartedly by our federal government, embarked on an unprecedented effort to dominate the world economy—especially the growing markets of Asia, Africa, and Latin America.

The global spread of American capital is about more than just cheap labor and free trade. Our corporations routinely dump their toxic waste on Third World soil. They blithely spearhead global warming. They arrogantly seek to dominate national cultures with their Hollywood films and their Disney theme parks. They greedily centralize world finances and peddle mountains of debt onto hapless developing nations. They unflinchingly churn out the bulk of the planet's deadly arms exports.

Meanwhile, Third World countries have been relegated to producing a larger and larger share of manufactured goods for world consumption at bargain-basement prices. There are more industrial jobs in the world than ever before, but the planet's industrial heartland has inexorably shifted away from the United States, Japan, and Europe toward Asia and Latin America. As it shifted, so did the path-breaking labor struggles of our era.

The globalization of capital, on the other hand, has produced its corollary—the globalization of labor. Since World War II, air travel has shortened physical distances and mass communications has diminished cultural differences. All the while, the wealth gap between the developed countries and the Third World has grown to a chasm. These phenomena have fueled unprecedented mass emigration to the United States and Western Europe, as displaced peasants and impoverished workers seek a share of the torrent of profits flowing to the rich nations. In the past, the old colonial ties meant that these immigrants gravitated to the metropolises of their former colonial masters.

The result has been a dramatic ethnic and racial transformation of the working classes of Europe and the United States. In Great Britain, burgeoning Pakistani, Indian, and Jamaican immigrant populations have unnerved native whites. In France, a right-wing movement has targeted Algerians and Tunisians,

Malians and Senegalese. In Germany, foreign nationals from Turkey, Africa, and Southeast Asia have drawn the ire of native citizens.

Here at home, unparalleled immigration has taken place with immigrants arriving from Mexico, the Caribbean, and Central and South America ever since World War II, their numbers escalating after immigration laws were liberalized in 1965. Over forty million foreigners settled here between 1960 and 2008, more than in any fifty-year span in the country's history, and half of those newcomers were from Latin America. The percentage of foreign-born people living in the United States is now the highest it's been since before the restrictive immigration laws of the 1920s. Yet most experts did not fully grasp the magnitude of the change despite a string of hyperbolic press accounts during the 1980s and 1990s that focused on Hispanic population growth.

By 2050, whites will cease to be a majority in the United States, though they will no doubt remain the dominant racial group in terms of wealth and power. It is likely that by the end of this century, a majority of the US population will trace its heritage to Latin America, not to Europe.

This is amazing when you consider that Latinos in the United States numbered a mere 9.1 million and represented just 4.5 percent of the population as recently as 1970. The Hispanic population explosion is no longer confined to the Southwest border region or to a handful of big states like California, New York, and Florida. It has now extended to virtually every suburb, small town, and rural area of the country, with Mexican restaurants, Spanish bodegas, and Latin music now a ubiquitous part of life throughout the USA.

Such rapid change has understandably led to deep insecurity among non-Hispanic whites, and even among some black Americans. This is especially so for baby boomers, who grew up during the 1950s and 1960s, when immigration rates were at the lowest levels of the twentieth century. The US foreign-born population was small then, and the prevalence of racial segregation and the proliferation of all-white suburbs meant that both white and black Americans had little social interaction with people who were culturally and linguistically different from themselves. The country, in other words, was racially divided but demographically homogenous.

Over the past few decades, immigrant workers have gradually become the heart and soul of the American labor movement. From Justice for Janitors in Southern California, to the hotel workers in Nevada and the hospital workers in New York, to the amazing growth of the Service Employees International Union, much of the progress of the labor movement can be traced to militancy among immigrant workers from Latin America and the Caribbean.

It was the 2006 wave of immigration protests, in fact, that revived May Day as a day of labor protest in the United States. Thus, progressives of all races must face the reality that any hope for fundamental change in US society rests largely on the shoulders of new immigrant labor. Those immigrants come from the very nations where the path-breaking struggles between capital and labor are now occurring. Like the Italian and Russian Jewish immigrant workers of the early twentieth century, they have not been co-opted by the crumbs of the US empire. Their condition makes it easier for them to understand the continuing conflict between workers of all countries and multinational capital.

They, more than any other sector of American workers, understand that just because the past is littered with numerous examples of failed socialist models, that doesn't mean workers must automatically accept the corrupt and oppressive system of capital that in 2008 plunged so much of the world into the greatest economic crisis since the Great Depression.

Over the past decade, trade unions, farmers, and indigenous workers in nearly a dozen Latin American countries have propelled that region toward amazing social progress. In Venezuela, Bolivia, Brazil, Peru, Chile, Ecuador, Uruguay, Paraguay, Guatemala, Nicaragua, and El Salvador, populist governments, many of them led by former leftist guerrillas and labor leaders, have swept into power through peaceful elections. Those new governments have broken free from the failed neoliberal economic policies long championed by Washington and Wall Street. Authoritarian governments run by generals and dictators are largely a thing of the past in Latin America. In several of those countries, the gap between rich and poor is diminishing rapidly. Government social programs and land reforms are lifting millions out of poverty. Those examples of real democratic reform and economic progress are not lost on the Latin American workers who were forced to leave their homeland and journey to El Norte.

Just as Latin America is today pointing the peoples of our planet toward a new era of popular democracy and a more just economic system, so, too, do Latin American immigrants in this country have the potential to point us toward a better world right here in the heart of the empire.

In saying this, I do not underestimate the difficulties involved. Unfortunately, millions of Americans today have been convinced by the most extensive propaganda system in history to identify with notions of our nation's God-given supremacy over the rest of the world (the theories of manifest destiny, of American exceptionalism, and even of white moral and racial supremacy over "less civilized" populations). In the short run, a deepening economic crisis—one sparked, perhaps, by economic collapse in Europe—is more likely to trigger a powerful right-wing, even neofascist movement, than resurgence of any socialist movement. But if the Occupy Wall Street phenomenon has taught us anything, it is that revolutionary movements often erupt at the most unexpected moments and in the most unlikely ways.

Unfortunately, the revolutionary spirit of Occupy will likely not spread beyond its original youth base until a few things occur. First, and most important, the beleaguered and crippled American trade union movement must be transformed into the main power center for immigrant workers. Too many trade unions today are controlled by old, white male leaders who have spent their whole lives accommodating capitalist power. That ossified generation must be convinced to retire, and the Latin Americans, other immigrants, African Americans, and women who make up the overwhelming bulk of their rank-and-file must seize control of their unions and revive them. Their unions must shed their historic arrogance and reimagine themselves as just a small part of the fast-growing international labor movement centered in places like China, India, Egypt, Brazil, and other parts of the developing world.

Second, leftists in America should stop propping up the bankrupt electoral system and instead challenge its domination by two political parties that are both financed by the nation's biggest corporations. They should foster third- and fourth-party movements, organizations that will have the potential for major growth during the next economic crisis and that might come to power in some cities or states and set an example of socialist governance.

Third, progressives should pay far more attention to creating and financing independent, noncommercial media systems that spread news, information, and progressive entertainment to tens of millions of Americans twenty-four hours a day, seven days a week. And they should do so not only in English, the nation's dominant language, but in Spanish, the second language of the United States, and in other minority languages, too.

In all three of these endeavors, Latin American immigrants can play a leading role, because many of them developed a more combative trade union spirit in their home countries, because many are accustomed to multiparty political systems back home, and because many grasp the importance of Spanish-language and other alternative media in spreading news and information to millions of "forgotten" people.

The next economic crisis is inevitable. That crisis will likely spawn a much stronger neofascist movement than most of us imagine. The rise of a radical, democratic, and socialist alternative is indeed possible, but only if American progressives appeal to the key groups of workers likely to rally to such a movement. Those key groups are not just African Americans; they are increasingly Latin American and Asian immigrants.

A better world is indeed possible, and those immigrant workers will point the way.

Chapter 14

Welfare in a New Society:
An End to Intentional Impoverishment
and Degradation

Frances Fox Piven

Most of the world is now in the grip of hyper-capitalism, what we call neoliberalism. This new system has brought us careening economic instabilities, worsening ecological disasters, brutal wars, a depleted public sector and poverty in the affluent global north, and the prospect of mass famine in the global south.

It seems high time to think about alternatives to the capitalist behemoth. I don't know whether we will ultimately call the new ways of organizing our society "socialist," but the values that have inspired movements for socialism in the past should inform our search. Those values include a society with sharply reduced inequalities in both material circumstances and social status. Socialist movements also aspire to lessen the grinding toil now imposed on those who work for wages. They dream of an inclusive culture. They fight for democratic practices and policies in which influence is widely shared. And they believe in eliminating the pervasive terror in everyday life that is produced by the exigencies of capitalist markets and the arbitrary power of the state regimes that support those markets.

No matter how successful the new society is in equalizing earnings and assets, however, we will have to be concerned about the potential for poverty and hard times. This might result from exogenous shocks, such as a drought or earthquakes, or from internal economic disorganization, including the instabilities produced by efforts to transform our institutions. Moreover, there will always be people who are not well suited to the work that is available because of their physical health or personal disorganization.

How our society treats these people is of great importance. Morally, it is important because it is unnecessary and cruel for an affluent society to impose impoverishment and humiliation on some of its members. It is less often recognized that the treatment of the poor has a large bearing on the well-being of the entire society.

The poverty policies characteristic of capitalist societies, especially the United States, form a template for what we should *not* do in the new society. They also suggest an agenda for constructing the institutions that will lead to a more equal, more democratic, and more humane society.

In *Regulating the Poor,* Richard Cloward and I argued that the treatment of the poor in modernizing Western societies could only be understood in relation to the problem of enforcing and regulating labor. That problem became more salient as labor markets supplanted the feudal system, which had shackled people to the soil and the lord. Of course, for much of our history, the majority of working people were poor. But we meant a stratum of people worse off than the main body of workers—people who had been stripped of social respect.

The system of discipline and assistance usually called "poor relief" dates from the early days of capitalism and industrialization. Relief systems were usually inaugurated after outbreaks of disorder by starving people. But their management was more importantly shaped by their role in disciplining workers. They gave meager assistance, and the terms of that assistance were harsh. Just as important, those who turned to the parish or the county for relief were subject to sustained rituals of public degradation.

That harsh treatment and degradation have always constituted a dramatic warning to the mass of working people trying to survive on their earnings. The practices of relief or the workhouse or welfare sent the message that there was a worse fate than low-wage work: to fall into abject poverty and become a pauper.

More recently, as China changed over to capitalism, it, too, developed programs similar to Anglo-American poor relief. The Chinese economy's astonishingly rapid growth in the past thirty years was made possible by the exploitation of masses of migrant workers from the countryside and what historian Peter Kwong calls the "systematic depreciation of the value of their labor." The old "iron rice bowl" system was dismantled, with programs supporting subsistence farmers cut back and urban workers' job security reduced.

As the older Chinese system of social benefits attached to employment disappeared, new programs were created, including one billed as a final resort for the most desperate of those laid off, most of whom were chronically ill or unskilled or disabled. The benefits offered were set by local authorities according to the Western principle of "less eligibility," which ensured that no one on the dole would receive as much as the worst-paid laborer. They were distributed in ways that morally stigmatized the recipients, much like our welfare system does.

Extreme poverty and its institutionalized insults have been used to divide and terrify working people for centuries. Now, with shrinking wages, work becoming more insecure and irregular, and the escalation of the war against unions, extreme poverty has again increased. So have its uses to intimidate the workers who are still managing to stay afloat. This strategy has been boldest in the United States. But while there are striking continuities in the law and practice of poor relief across time and across borders, the institution has also been periodically overhauled, sometimes to respond to popular rebelliousness, and sometimes reflecting deep-seated changes in labor markets.

In this neoliberal era, wages and labor conditions have been deteriorating worldwide, as workers in the developed world are pitted against desperately impoverished workers everywhere. Recent cutbacks in the so-called safety net in the United States reflect this. These cutbacks also take into account the vastly expanded domestic pool of wage laborers which include most women, as well as large numbers of African Americans and Latinos after they were displaced from traditional agriculture.

The results have been brutal. And the situation of the poor in the United States is worse than the official poverty figures suggest. For example, in 2006, interest payments on consumer debt put over four million people who were not officially in poverty below the line, making them debt poor. Similarly, if child-care costs, estimated at over $5,000 a year in 2002, were deducted from gross income, many more people would be counted as officially poor. The numbers would be higher still if homeless working people, adult children living with their parents, and doubled-up families had to pay full housing costs.

The United States also employs a different and harsher measure of poverty than most other countries. In the United States, the official poverty line is an absolute measure of subsistence needs. It's simply three times the income needed to cover a minimal food budget, one created in 1959 and adjusted for inflation in food costs. Most countries, however, measure poverty in relative terms, generally counting people as poor if they make less than half the median income—thus comparing the circumstances of those at the bottom with the society's overall living standards.

If poverty is measured that way, the United States has far higher poverty rates than other rich countries. Indeed, poverty rates in the United States may be comparable to those in some parts of the global south. The poverty rate in New York City is just under 20 percent. If New York City were a nation, reports James Parrott, "its level of income concentration would rank fifteenth among 134 countries, between Chile and Honduras." Wall Street is less than 10 miles from the Bronx, the nation's poorest urban county.

Some of this is the result of the rising unemployment and reductions in take-home pay associated with the Great Recession. But it also reflects the high levels of poverty in the United States before the economic meltdown of 2007–2009. In the six years preceding that, the poverty rate actually increased for the first time on record during an economic recovery, from 11.7 percent in 2001 to 12.5 percent in 2007. Poverty rates for single mothers in 2007 were 50 percent higher in the United States than in fifteen other high-income countries. Black employment rates and income were declining *before* the recession struck in 2007. And there is simply no evidence to support the familiar bromide that poverty in the United States today is a temporary condition associated with youth or hard luck. Our national myths notwithstanding, the United States is a low-mobility society.

Another cause of high and rising poverty levels is the decades-long business mobilization to reduce labor costs and weaken labor organizations in the workplace. That mobilization began in the 1970s, when employers trying to hold down wages became much more intransigent in negotiations. Since then, they've busted unions and restructured the labor process to make work more insecure. Business also mobilized to change government labor policies, resulting in National Labor Relations Board decisions much less favorable to workers and unions. Workplace regulations were not enforced. The minimum wage lagged far behind inflation. Safety-net programs for the unemployed or the unemployable became more restrictive, and benefit levels fell—although the Earned Income Tax Credit, which effectively provides a taxpayer subsidy to low-earning workers and their employers, expanded enormously.

Inevitably, this campaign to reduce labor's share of national earnings increased the proportion of the population unable to earn even a poverty-level livelihood. But the programs that provided assistance to the poor were singled out for especially steep cutbacks, and the poor themselves were singled out in a sustained campaign of venomous insult. A host of new think tanks, political organizations, and lobbyists in Washington carried the message that the country's problems were caused by the poor, whose shiftlessness and sexual promiscuity were being indulged by a too-generous welfare system.

By the election of Ronald Reagan as president in 1980, this propaganda had smoothed the path for huge cuts in programs for poor people. Means-tested programs (such as food stamps, Medicaid, and Aid to Families with Dependent Children) were cut by 54 percent, job training by 81 percent, housing assistance by 47 percent. These cuts accumulated to erode the safety net that protected workers too, especially low-wage workers, who were primarily women and racial minorities.

By the 1990s, the Democrats had largely joined the Republican campaign against the poor and blacks, as they floundered for electoral strategies to ward off the worst of the Republican demands and to raise campaign funds from business. It was Bill Clinton who campaigned with the slogan "End welfare as we know it."

Much of this effort was played out in state politics as well, with cutbacks in the Aid to Families with Dependent Children

(AFDC) and state-level general assistance programs. AFDC was a federal grant-in-aid program targeted to impoverished single mothers and their children. It ceded considerable authority to the states, and often the counties, to set benefit levels and determine who was eligible.

When black insurgency escalated in the 1960s, the federal government issued a series of rulings that restrained state and local governments from their customarily restrictive welfare practices. Not surprisingly, the rolls rose; benefit levels reached their peak in the late 1960s. Then, as the protests subsided, federal oversight was withdrawn. Between 1970 and 1996, the average level of maximum benefits fell by more than half when adjusted for inflation, to the point where the income they provided for a family of three was well below the poverty line.

Finally, in 1996, the AFDC program was eliminated, to be replaced by Temporary Assistance to Needy Families (TANF), a block grant that gave the states almost total leeway to limit access to assistance, and also to steadily reduce benefit levels for those who received it. The law also gave the states a remarkable incentive to limit assistance, since they received the full amount of federal funding regardless of how many people were on the rolls or the benefits they received.

If we want to strive for better policies in a transformed society, at least three principles must be observed. First, we should try to provide at least a subsistence-level income for everyone. Obviously, this would hugely benefit the poor, as many impoverished people are not helped at all by current assistance programs, and the ones who do get aid receive such meager benefits that they remain desperately poor. For example, the maximum benefit for a family of three lucky enough to receive Temporary Assistance to Needy Families in New York City is now $577 a month, far below the cost of renting even a squalid and tiny apartment, with nothing left over for other expenses.

It would not only be the very poor who would benefit from an income guarantee. The old English principle of "less eligibility" was based on the understanding that relief benefits set a kind of floor below which wages could not fall, for the simple reason that many people might then forsake work for relief. The implications of this logic are clear. A guaranteed income not conditioned on work would strengthen the market power of low-wage workers. It would have a liberating effect on many other workers as well. Not only would it reduce the pervasive anxiety caused by fear of losing your job, but at least some of these working people could take advantage of the new income guarantee to explore different endeavors, to try their hand at a new trade, to learn music or write poetry, to develop hitherto untapped potentials for creativity. A transformed society should aim to free people from material anxiety and the tyranny of wage slavery. And if it did, the results would contribute to continuing the process of transformation.

Second, as we know from the experience with American programs to support the poor, income-support policies would confront opposition from both employers and people animated simply by envy and anxiety. So we would need to anchor our income guarantee firmly to garner popular support. This would require more than declaring that income supports should be a matter of right. "Rights" are too easily subverted or ignored. The best way to anchor the guarantee would be by making it universal, applying not only to all citizens but to all residents of the country.

The reason for this last proviso is key. If we exclude permanent immigrants from our income protections (as we now do in a number of programs) we would still have large numbers of people in poverty, as we do now—except that they would all have foreign names.

Finally, a universal income-support program should be administered with a minimum of interaction between the people who receive the supports and the bureaucracy responsible for distributing them. Checks could be mailed, or funds deposited in accounts electronically. That would eliminate the opportunities for systematic degradation associated with welfare programs in the past.

Where would the money come from? The United States is a fabulously rich society. We can afford to fight endless wars across the globe, and at home we let the wealthy cannibalize government and our communities. Even so, we are not as a people so badly off. Social transformation in the pursuit of equality, inclusion, democracy, and social justice requires that we find ways to take back the wealth stolen from ordinary people here and elsewhere by capitalist elites, especially the wealth stolen from those who are the worst off among us.

Chapter 15

Food for All: Creating a Socially Sustainable Food System

Arun Gupta

Open your refrigerator and you've opened a door to the world: coffee from Ethiopia, shrimp from Thailand, blueberries from Chile, apples from New Zealand, spices from the Middle East, and ground beef that may have bits of meat from cattle raised in several different countries. For those who can afford it, the global cornucopia is one of the wonders of capitalism. Those who can't suffer starvation and hunger, displacement from the land, and the disappearance of their unique cultures. And all of humanity must bear the costs of industrialized agriculture, including global warming, depleted soils, species extinction, leveled forests, collapsing ocean life, and the diseases of obesity and malnutrition.

The immediate cause of our broken food system is overproduction. Capitalism demands endless expansion. More production and more trade mean capitalists can generate more profits by capturing a bigger share of the market and driving down costs. Inevitably, this floods the market with goods. The excess supply drives down prices and profits, which the capitalist addresses by shuttering factories, squeezing wages, and firing workers. For farmers, a glut of wheat or pork means they earn less. They desperately try to stay afloat by slashing prices and producing more, which further depresses prices.

A socialist agricultural system could eliminate such crises, but it would still have to produce a surplus of food and agricultural goods. Food is different from other necessities. While people can weather a housing shortage by doubling up in households, and limited medical care can be addressed by delaying noncritical procedures and using other therapies, a food shortage spells hunger or death for many.

With store shelves bursting with beans, bread, and fruit—and a hot pizza just a phone call away—we take our food system for granted. In fact, it is fragile. If farmers lack seeds, tractors, fuel, or fertilizer, not enough crops will be planted. Diseases, pests, and unpredictable weather affect harvests. There are losses all along the supply chain, from rotting grain in silos to crushed boxes of crackers in warehouses, from sour milk in supermarkets to mushy vegetables in your fridge. To top it off, global warming is bringing with it its own disasters, like the drought that ravaged much of the American breadbasket in 2012.

Under capitalism, the system favors large agribusinesses that can mobilize economies of scale and public subsidies to their advantage. Although farm subsidies are supposed to help "family farmers," corporations vacuum up most of them. In 2008, a US Department of Agriculture study found that the largest 12 percent of farms raked in 62 percent of the subsidies.

Public subsidies squeeze farmers' incomes by forcing the price of many commodities below the cost of production. Also, giant food corporations such as Cargill, Tyson, Archer Daniels Midland (ADM), and Kraft create choke points by controlling key parts of the system, such as soybean crushing, dairy processing, and beef packing. These two forces—below-cost prices for foodstuffs and monopoly control of processing and trading—spell doom for small farmers. Processors and traders pay farmers such low wholesale prices that only the heavily subsidized big farms can consistently turn a profit. Small farmers have few other options, because a handful of corporations have sway over the markets for each specific agricultural product.

As a result, millions of small farmers go bankrupt and are pushed off the land, and large enterprises expand their control of the market. When the North American Free Trade Agreement (NAFTA) went into effect in 1994, Mexicans were told that it would reduce the price of corn tortillas, the most important food in their diet. By 2006, as heavily subsidized American corn flooded Mexico, corn prices had plunged by 59 percent. Despite all this cheap corn, tortilla prices leaped by more than 42 percent in 2007.

What happened? A few corporations, including Cargill, ADM, and Walmart, gained control of key nodes in the corn industry including wet milling, producing corn flour, tortilla making, and retailing. Traders profit by buying corn when it's priced low, hoarding it, and then selling it when prices rise. Walmart captured 30 percent of all supermarket grocery sales in Mexico. That enabled it to raise prices to increase its profits or lower them to force out small retailers.

Some governments subsidize the entire agricultural sector rather than just large for-profit farms. But most people still lose out. Some subsidies push up the price of food. Sometimes the government dumps surplus food purchased from large producers into the market, imperiling small farmers and peddlers. Big food companies gobble up low-cost inputs to create unhealthy processed foods. Familiar foods and ways of eating are sacrificed on the altar of profit—chips and soda eaten on the run replace beans and rice eaten as part of a communal meal. Small-scale retailers, producers, and distributors are swallowed up or forced out of the industrial-scale system.

The motor of capitalism is to turn the stuff of life—bread, water, housing, medicine, education—into market commodities. Its intent is not to fill people's bellies, which is why an estimated 925 million people worldwide suffer from hunger despite the sea of abundance.

The use of food crops as a raw material for industry also diverts food from people's mouths. Corn, America's number-one crop by yield, is used in scores of other products, including plastics, paint, insecticides, pharmaceuticals, solvents, rayon, antifreeze, soap, biofuel, and animal feed. In Mexico, the use of corn for biofuel is a significant factor in rising tortilla prices, and thus in declining consumption. About one-eighth of Mexican children under the age of five are chronically malnourished.

Under a socialist system, food would be a right, not a commodity. But if socialism is defined as state ownership, then the state will be tempted to commodify agricultural goods as an easy means to secure hard currency or pay for critical supplies if desperate. In Cuba in the late 1980s, sugar accounted for 70 percent of the country's export earnings, as it would trade the Soviet Union one ton of sugar for 4.5 tons of crude oil.

Two other aspects of commodification need to be addressed under socialism: land and labor. Mexico's *ejido* system of common lands did not break up the plantations or prevent the spread of landless agricultural workers because large landholders, especially cattle ranchers, used their economic power to increase their holdings. And even in a socialist state, commodifying food leads to the industrial-scale farming that's prevalent under capitalism. This turns many farmers into rural wage laborers and undermines food security for producers, individuals, communities, and nations. It certainly abandons the socialist ideal that workers control the means of production.

In a genuine socialist system, in which agricultural workers, farmers, and communities control the land, farming, processing, and distribution, the imperative for commodification would be reduced because much of the food would be consumed locally. But as very few regions, especially those with large populations, can meet the nutritional needs of all inhabitants, trading is a necessity. This requires systems of exchange.

What would a socialist food system look like? Land would be collectively owned, not just by farmers but by everyone in the community. It would not be privately owned under any circumstances. (The use of land could change, but that would be democratically decided.) Those who work the land would receive an equal share of the proceeds, while those in the community who depend on that land for sustenance but do not perform agricultural work would also have a right to foodstuffs. They would have a say in decisions about land use, what is produced, and how surpluses are distributed.

In cities and towns, vacant lots could be used as community farms. In the United States during World War II, it's estimated that "victory gardens" grew as much produce as commercial agriculture, with nearly ten million tons of fruit and vegetables harvested annually from rooftops, window planters, and empty lots.

Americans saved this food by canning it, which allows food to be stored in glass jars at room temperature for up to a year. This requires canning equipment, knowledge, labor, time, and facilities. In northern regions, where outdoor growing seasons last six months or less, the average family would have to grow, process, can, and store a few hundred jars in order to have fruits and vegetables year-round. Multiply that by a few thousand households in a small town, and the scale of production quickly becomes industrial.

To create a local, collective food system, we would have to rethink daily life, from housing and community to work and leisure, so people would have the time and space to farm. Common gardens are more efficient than individual plots because the community can combine labor and resources. At harvest time, communal kitchens would be vital to prepping, cooking, and canning the hundreds of tons of raw food. Individual households would not have to mobilize extra labor or own canning equipment that they'd use only a few times a year. Communal kitchens could also feed households, workplaces, and schools year-round.

As socialism is about social relations, any new food system would have to place a high priority on its communal aspects. The food- and nutrition-related diseases that afflict affluent countries like the United States start with alienation. Many farmers say children today are often unable to distinguish an apple from a tomato or a horse from a cow. Without such basic knowledge, children are more apt to believe chicken nuggets, chips, and candy bars are real food.

In addition to communal gardens and kitchens, there would be cooperatives for distribution. One example is Brooklyn's Park Slope Food Coop, the largest US-based food cooperative where all members work. Community-supported agriculture, in which a group of people receive food directly from a farm, cutting out wasteful middlemen, is another successful form of collective distribution.

Some people would be happy to grow and process as much of their own food as possible. This would require dramatically scaling back the workweek. For those unable or not inclined to farm, agricultural work would become part of the commons. Workers in food production would receive other means of subsistence— such as housing, clothing, health care, transportation, and education—in exchange for the fruits of their labor. Workers in non-agricultural sectors could also help plant and harvest crops or work in the distribution or production process, trading labor instead of money for food.

Schools would produce food to feed students and to educate children about healthy eating habits, humanity's connection with nature, and the social roles of food. The "farm-to-school" model could connect individual farms with schools, so children could learn about cultivation hands-on. Communal kitchens would teach children and adults how to prepare and cook food, and could also teach about different peoples' food cultures and traditions.

With most households of just one or two people, most of us in the workforce are pressed for time to prepare food. The quick fix is to stuff our faces with processed foods, which are engineered to light up our pleasure centers like a video game. Corporations profit at the expense of our individual and social health. In societies where communal meals are still the norm, such as in France, rates of obesity-related diseases are much lower because people snack less and eat less junk and industrial foods (though that is changing for younger generations in France).

Space is one of the most important issues in any economy. Local agriculture can provide some protein and fat in the form of aquaculture and egg-laying chickens and ducks, but the cultivation of many foods—grains, nuts, legumes, vegetable oils, beef, pork, fish, spices, tea, chocolate, coffee, salt, and sugar—requires specialized equipment, labor, climates, and land. This makes it impractical or impossible to grow them in urban areas.

Questions of land and labor are more challenging when a few regions, such as central China's rice paddies, southern Ukraine's wheat fields, or the American Great Plains, account for a large share of global food production. Control of the land should be in the public domain, but how will that work if tens or even hundreds of millions of people depend on a specific "breadbasket" for sustenance?

To some degree, production can be dispersed and traditional crops substituted. For example, for many urban dwellers in Nigeria, bread has displaced traditional starches like sorghum, millet, and yams. Nigeria is now the world's leading importer of US wheat—3.3 million tons in 2010. It would not be technically difficult for Nigeria to switch back, but the biggest obstacle might be changing bread-eating habits.

Nonetheless, trade is desirable. Many would find it a cruel world to live in without coffee, wine, spices, and chocolate. The question is how to do it. Flying flowers from Colombia or fish from Japan to New York City is ecologically destructive, displaces traditional crops, and relies on exploited labor—from the workers picking crops in toxic conditions to the ones retailing them in poverty-wage jobs. Non-perishable goods can be moved by ship and rail, which are far more energy-efficient than jet planes. Many types of produce, such as bananas, citrus fruit, apples, and tubers, can also be transported over long distances by these slower and more sustainable methods.

Every political system must grapple with how to allocate finite agricultural inputs such as energy, water, seeds, fertilizer, machinery, chemicals, and knowledge. (Under capitalism, food has itself become an input, whether as grain to bulk up cattle or sugarcane that is refined into ethanol.) After World War II, when countries that proclaimed socialism promoted state-led development, the farmers who received the most inputs were men producing for export markets, rather than women who were growing food for household and internal consumption. Sociologist Philip McMichael writes of this era, "Only monetized transactions were counted as productive, devaluing subsistence, cooperative labor, indigenous culture, seed saving, and managing the commons as unproductive, marginalized, and undeveloped activity."

If hard-cash exports are a priority, agriculture will evolve into a capitalist system regardless of the governing ideology. If community were the priority, then dependence on the market would decrease. But what is community? If a poor rice harvest in the Philippines means rice has to be imported from Thailand, or if Russia needs wheat and only the United States has enough reserves, the shortages increase the likelihood of war or civil unrest. Indeed, the 2011 democratic uprising in Egypt was stoked by high food prices.

In India, for more than a millennium prior to British colonialism, famines occurred less than once a century because villages had abundant food reserves—to which everyone in the village had a right—to get them through a poor harvest. Fifty years ago, many governments practiced similar forms of collective support by providing marketing boards, price supports, grain reserves, roads, subsidized seeds and fertilizers, rural credit, tariffs, export barriers, and other types of aid that made episodes of mass starvation rare. The main goal was food security: each country should be secure in its food supply.

In the 1980s, a new ideology replaced that one: the market will provide for all. "The idea that developing countries should feed themselves is an anachronism from a bygone era," a Reagan administration official declared. "They could better ensure their food security by relying on US agricultural products, which are available in most cases at lower cost." This official neglected to mention that low-cost US products were available for sale to those developing countries thanks to US government subsidies to US farmers.

This double standard has not stopped Washington, its allies, and the World Trade Organization and International Monetary Fund from leveraging aid and loans to force countries in Asia, Africa, and Latin America to stop supporting their own local agriculture. The West demands that less-developed countries turn to export goods to generate foreign currency, and many countries comply because they are drowning in debt that can only be paid back with dollars or euros. This has led to a situation, now common, even in the United States, for many areas to have abundant food while nearby communities struggle with widespread hunger and malnutrition.

The notion of "food security," whether in the US or developing countries, was problematic, as it relied on a state-centered system intended to maximize food production. This favored an industrial model, such as the "Green Revolution" of the 1960s, an agricultural technique introduced to developing countries by the US that pushed many subsistence farmers off the land. The Green Revolution also relied on toxic pesticides and artificial fertilizers that made countries and farmers more dependent on the large Western corporations that produced them. It was only a few steps from there to growing genetically modified crops. And it is highly questionable whether using these artificial inputs increases food production.

A new grassroots democratic model is known as "food sovereignty." It is based "on a farmer-driven agriculture that is the key to food-secure relations of environmental and social sustainability." The concept was developed by Via Campesina, which describes itself as an international peasant movement. Via Campesina states:

> In order to guarantee the independence and food sovereignty of all of the world's peoples, it is essential that food be produced through diversified, farmer-based production systems. Food sovereignty is the right of peoples to define their own agriculture and food policies, to protect and regulate domestic agricultural production and trade in order to achieve sustainable development objectives, to determine the extent to which they want to be self-reliant, and to restrict the dumping of products in their markets. Food sovereignty does not negate trade, but rather, it promotes the formulation of trade policies and practices that serve the rights of peoples to safe, healthy, and ecologically sustainable production.

Such a vision incorporates trade, but it makes it secondary to security and democratic control for and by the people, not for state, corporate, or other elite interests. It recognizes there is no one-size-fits-all solution, which was one of the fatal flaws of the state-led socialist model of industrialized agriculture. As famed French farmer-activist Jose Bove puts it, "We have to provide answers at different levels—not just the international level, but local and national levels, too."

Creating a socially and ecologically sustainable food system means confronting the power and complexity of capitalism. Growing tomatoes in a city plot or raising a few chickens in your backyard is not a solution. Neither is shopping at Whole Foods or a farmers market, no matter how much personal satisfaction you get by doing so. We can't repair our food system by trying to shop our way to a greener planet.

A socialist food system would mimic both the complexity and simplicity of nature. It would create many different forms to meet the needs and conditions in different communities and regions. It would act according to the fundamental principles of democratic control over the economy and people's right to have nutritious and sufficient food.

These questions will become ever more urgent as global warming wreaks havoc on the biosphere. Humanity will have to figure out how to band together to ensure a just life for all or risk descending further into barbarism. This is a struggle that we can win—one that we *must* win.

Chapter 16

The Right to Housing

Tom Angotti

Wall Street and entrenched real estate interests caused the 2008 financial collapse and today's deep recession. Homeowners were stuck with huge mortgage debt and declining house values, and many are being foreclosed upon and evicted. Renters are suffering from lower wages and lost jobs, and many can't afford to pay their landlords. More people are homeless.

But if capitalism messed up, how would a whole new economic system like socialism be any different? Couldn't it make things worse? Isn't the United States destined to stay the world's leading capitalist power? Thanks to Occupy Wall Street and the long tradition of protest and opposition that preceded it, we can now entertain the notion that capitalism isn't eternal and that another system is possible.

If you get rid of the big banks, insurance companies, real estate moguls, and everyone else who profits from housing, you'll have a much better chance of paying your bills, keeping your home, and staying in your neighborhood. Get rid of these corporate thieves, and we'll put an end to the constant cycle of boom and bust in which our homes and neighborhoods are chips in a giant casino.

The Right to Housing

First and foremost, a socialist housing system has to treat housing as a basic human right, not a thing to be bought and sold for profit. And it's not just the right to a roof over your head in any old place. It is the right to a decent living environment, including basic public services like health care, education, heat, water, and public space. It is the right to live anywhere in the city, the right to strong bonds with your neighbors and family, and the right to protection from eviction or foreclosure.

Americans are regularly thrown out of their homes. Foreclosures and evictions are treated as normal and necessary. But they can and should be eliminated. Because land and housing are treated as commodities, people who happen to live in locations desirable to real estate investors are forced out of their homes because they can't afford the rising costs that result from real estate speculation. Banks and investors also speculate with our mortgages, which they exploit for as much as they can get.

A socialist alternative will protect homeowners and tenants from displacement and eviction. No homeowners will be put out on the street because they can't make monthly payments to banks and insurance companies. No tenants will be evicted because they couldn't pay the rent after they lost their job. Nobody will be forced out of their community because some developer, with or without the backing of government, wants their land so they can build luxury condos or a shopping mall. When land and housing are instead seen as public goods, like health care and education, there will be no place for the speculators who roam the country looking for bargains so they can evict working people, flip properties, and sell them to wealthy buyers. A socialist housing system will have to eliminate private profit and establish housing as a basic human right.

Racism and Exclusion

Another deep flaw in the capitalist housing system is that it has fostered racism and racial segregation in our towns and cities. A socialist alternative is based on full equality for all, so that no one will be excluded from buying or renting based on their race or ethnicity. Real estate brokers who steer whites to white neighborhoods and blacks to black neighborhoods have to be put out of business. Indeed, the entire real estate industry should be shut down so that rent and housing costs don't depend on the neighborhood you live in but rather on your ability to pay. The quality of your local schools shouldn't depend on how much you can pay in local property taxes, and all Americans should be guaranteed access to education no matter where they live.

Defenders of the current system point to the gaping inequalities in our cities as the result of personal life choices. But the socialist principle makes it possible for people to have *more* choices. By sharply reducing the huge gap in incomes, we will also narrow the huge gap in housing costs that limits where most people can afford to live in our cities and suburbs.

Defenders of the current system will also tell you that socialism won't work, that housing will get run down because there will be no incentive for anyone to maintain it or build new housing. These are the same people who tell us that government regulation and tenants' rights—not their own disinvestment in our neighborhoods—make things worse. They say socialism is against private ownership of housing and is bound to lead to a monstrous and incompetent government monopoly.

A socialist housing system doesn't necessarily mean that the government will own everything. And even if it did own and maintain all housing, that by itself wouldn't make it socialist. In many socialist countries during the twentieth century, individuals owned their houses and apartments while government owned the land on which they were built. For over fifty years, since the Cuban Revolution's urban reform nationalized land and eliminated real estate speculation, all Cubans have owned their own homes. Indeed, homeownership under socialism can be just another way of guaranteeing the right to housing. Individual ownership is allowed, although limited and regulated, while government retains the rights to land.

Socialism is about creating a new society based on equality, human welfare, and cooperation instead of competition. In fact, once the banks, insurance companies, and landlords are out of the picture, there can be many ownership models. It doesn't matter who has the legal title if everyone is guaranteed the right to housing and land is protected from real estate speculation. There could be individual private owners, cooperatives, condominiums, government housing, factory-owned housing, community land trusts, and other forms of ownership. But the land itself would always remain in the public domain and couldn't be bought and sold on the market. We should learn from and consciously move toward a system much like that of the indigenous Americans (whose land was stolen by European settlers)—a system that honors and respects the land as sacred instead of treating it like a commodity. If we see ourselves as the collective stewards of land, we will want to treat it better and work with our neighbors to protect it.

Nonetheless, taking housing out of the marketplace won't by itself guarantee decent housing. Somebody has to build, operate, and maintain it, and all of that costs money. The alternative to the capitalist housing system can't be collapsing buildings and run-down neighborhoods. So we'll still have to pay, both as individuals and communities, to have decent housing. Government can only do so much, and we know that big government agencies don't do very well when it comes to managing things at the local level.

There are many different ways to organize the housing system so that individuals, communities, and local governments can work out their differences and cooperate. No doubt, individual households should be responsible for the upkeep of their own housing units, whether they are single-family homes or apartments. Beyond that, cooperatives, neighborhood associations, and local authorities could take responsibility at the neighborhood and community level. They should all be community-based, because the bigger the area, the harder it is to coordinate decent services. We need to strengthen community institutions because they will have to fill the void left by landlords and banks. But government at all levels will have to be involved to finance new housing, set regulations, and prevent the reemergence of speculators and landlords.

While our communities should be able to operate and maintain housing, we'll probably have to turn to our state and federal governments for the large investments needed to build new housing. The government now subsidizes private developers, who favor the most expensive housing because that's where they can make the most money. The government also subsidizes "affordable housing," which most people can't afford—and which makes private developers richer as well. For example, in New York City, developers who build luxury housing can get government subsidies if 20 percent of the apartments are "affordable"—affordable, that is, to households making as much as $120,000 a year. A socialist government, however, would set as its first priority building new housing for people who need it the most—the millions of people who are now homeless or close to being homeless. A government not tied to the giant homebuilding industry would also be able to meet the need for new housing by taking over the huge supply of empty housing units currently kept off the market by speculators.

Socialism would not, of course, be some kind of magical paradise on Earth where everyone automatically receives a penthouse and is able to do whatever he or she wants with it. Some problems could get worse, and entirely new housing problems will emerge. Here the experiences of the socialist countries since the 1917 Bolshevik Revolution are informative. The twentieth-century socialists ended most evictions and dispossession, built an enormous amount of new housing, founded new cities, and successfully linked housing with jobs. They proved that decent and truly affordable housing could be built without a private market. But maintenance was a persistent problem, and too often huge government bureaucracies with a top-down leadership and with limited budgets let housing fall into disrepair. This was a new and distinctly bureaucratic socialist housing problem, and it contributed to the public dissatisfaction that led to the collapse of the Soviet Union. There were also shortages of housing for larger families and singles, and divorced couples sometimes had to wait years to get separate apartments. Stability and freedom from the threat of displacement are important, but they need to be balanced with the need for mobility.

Twenty-first-century socialism will have to learn from the mistakes of the past and find new ways to engage individuals in truly democratic local governance. Everyone should participate in and take responsibility for their community and environment. This will be a lot of work. The human right to housing is not an open license for individuals to abuse the public trust; everyone must shoulder some responsibility for such a system to work.

We will need to invent new methods for allocating housing throughout metropolitan areas, methods that don't depend on how much money people have, although a socialist economy will presumably eliminate the huge gap between the 99 percent and the 1 percent. We will need to find a democratic solution that opens up the exclusive enclaves of wealth and improves the quality of life in working-class communities of color. Eliminating the extremes of rich and poor neighborhoods will also make it easier for people to find housing near their jobs and reduce the economic, environmental, and personal costs of commuting.

There will be many conflicts, but equality, not some romantic utopia, is the goal. Building stable, diverse local communities based on inclusion and equality is both a socialist ideal and possibility.

Chapter 17

Socialized Medicine Means Everyone Gets Care, Regardless of Whether They Have Money

Dave Lindorff

When I was a young man just getting started on my career in journalism, I lived in New York City. My wife, Joyce, a harpsichordist, was herself just starting out as a freelance musician. We had a cheap but rather minimal health insurance plan that didn't pay for doctor or emergency room visits—only for very costly hospital stays, and then only 80 percent of the total bill. One day, Joyce, who suffers from allergies, had a severe asthma attack—her breathing became increasingly labored. We rushed out of our apartment, hailed a taxi to Roosevelt Hospital, and went into the emergency room entrance.

Joyce was gasping so hard she couldn't talk, but I was nonetheless questioned at length by an intake nurse about our insurance plan and our finances. It was clear to everyone around us that Joyce was in danger of losing consciousness because the swelling in her throat had constricted her windpipe, but the intake process dragged on as she gasped for breath. The hospital, a private institution, like most hospitals in this country, wanted to make sure it would get paid before it would admit her for treatment!

I lost my temper and began yelling and making a scene. Another nurse came by, saw Joyce's condition, and, fortunately, brought her in to be seen by a doctor before the financial details were resolved. She was given a drug to reduce the swelling, and she recovered. We ended up paying the hospital $700 for this abusive nightmare.

Today, things have only gotten worse. The nearly 50 million people in America who don't have health insurance—and that number keeps growing as employers eliminate their insurance plans for workers—have nowhere to turn when they or their families get sick.

Think about that number. There are just over 310 million Americans: nearly one in six is uninsured. Many people with curable ailments have died for lack of care. That's what happened to a teenage boy brought to a hospital by police in Chicago. He died on the sidewalk as the cops stood by helplessly: the hospital wouldn't admit him because he had no insurance.

America is the only modern industrial nation in the world that does this to its people. Everywhere else—Japan, Germany, Spain, Italy, Australia, Canada, Taiwan—there is some kind of system through which every single person has easy access not only to emergency care but to doctors and hospitals as well. In most of these countries, the patient receiving care pays nothing or merely a token fee. The cost is borne by the whole population, which finances the system through taxation.

These countries use several different health care models. The United Kingdom has a truly socialist-style National Health Service. In the British system, doctors are on salary from the national government, which also owns the hospitals. Canada's Medicare system is semi-socialist; the various provinces each pay private hospitals and doctors a set fee for providing care. In

Switzerland, the government establishes a basic health insurance plan that all insurance companies must offer to all citizens at a fixed cost. The insurance companies are not allowed to make a profit on these policies, but wealthier citizens are free to buy costlier insurance with better benefits, if they prefer. Amazingly, all of these models cost individuals, families, and society at large far less than health care in the United States.

In the UK, when people get sick—whether with strep throat or AIDS—they don't have to worry about how they will pay for their care: there is no cost for treatment. In Ontario, Canada, if the son of a top executive at General Motors Canada breaks his leg playing hockey, he is rushed to a hospital, where he is taken care of for free. If the daughter of an unemployed Haitian immigrant in Toronto gets hurt playing soccer, she'll be treated for free, too, under the same Medicare system. Both kids might even be treated by the same doctor in the same emergency room.

The British, Swiss, and Canadians have better access to primary medical care as well. And because diseases are generally easier to treat and more easily cured when they are diagnosed early, they are able to remain in better health.

But in the American system, only those who have good health insurance plans—generally government workers or staff at large corporations that must offer generous benefits packages in order to attract top-notch employees—can easily afford to go to the doctor whenever they are sick. A doctor's visit usually costs a nominal fee called a "co-pay"—no more than $20 or $30. When they are sick, they can be treated immediately. If they are becoming seriously or chronically ill, they can be referred to a specialist or sent to the hospital right away, improving their chances of recovery.

But many Americans, even those who have some kind of health insurance plan, don't have adequate access to health care. Instead, they might be responsible for paying perhaps the first $1,000 of their medical bills out of their own pocket before any insurance reimbursements kick in. That poses a terrible dilemma for a family in such a situation. If you feel a sore throat coming on, do you go to the doctor and pay perhaps $75 or $100 for an office visit? Or do you wait to see if it goes away on its own because you need that money to buy groceries? If you decide to wait and you have not a cold but strep throat, not only do you become very sick, but your family may get sick, too.

I was in that kind of situation when I was thirty-six and my daughter was a baby. She had a condition called febrile seizure syndrome. If she got sick and ran a high fever, she'd have a seizure and stop breathing, sometimes for as long as two minutes. It was horrifying to see. Her little body would stiffen and turn blue, and her eyes would roll back in her head. Once we learned about her condition, we would always rush her to the pediatrician at the first sign of a higher than normal temperature.

But each of those visits cost us $75, and my wife and I didn't have much money at the time. Sometimes, when she got sick, I remember thinking, "Oh, maybe this is just a flu, and visiting the pediatrician won't help. I'll just give her Tylenol and try to keep her cool with a wet washcloth so she doesn't have a seizure." Then I'd start to feel guilty: "But what if this is a bacterial infection, and the doctor could treat it?" Usually we'd relent and take her to the doctor—and spend $75 to find out that it was just a cold. Parents should never have to consider money in such situations. And in a society with socialized medical care, they wouldn't have to.

In a socialist society, a parent with a sick baby could go straight to the doctor, or in an emergency, to the hospital. The baby wouldn't be at risk of suffering through something potentially life-threatening, and the parents wouldn't have to face the financial anxiety of deciding to see a doctor—or suffer the guilt of not seeing one.

For those fifty million Americans with no insurance, the situation is worse still. They are usually poor, and therefore often choose not to see a doctor when they are sick. Doctors in America are private businesspeople, and most of them demand payment before they'll see a patient no matter how sick that person is. So poor people often wait until they are so sick that they must go to a hospital emergency room. Such facilities are generally required by law to admit anyone who needs treatment.

But many American hospitals have eliminated their emergency rooms, so that they don't have to accept patients who walk in off the street. Such hospitals only admit those referred by a private doctor. So the uninsured must find a hospital with a public emergency room; in rural areas, that can mean a drive of over fifty miles. Even these hospitals sometimes turn uninsured sick or injured people away. Stories of people dying after being sent away from hospital emergency rooms are legion.

To address the soaring number of uninsured Americans, the administration of President Barack Obama introduced, and Congress passed, the Affordable Care Act of 2010, dubbed "Obamacare" by its critics, a name subsequently adopted by the administration itself. Starting in 2014, health insurance companies must sell policies to anyone who can afford them, business owners with more than fifty employees must provide minimal health insurance for them or pay a fine, and those who do not receive insurance through their workplace must buy it on their own or be fined at tax time.

But the available plans will be costly (the law's price controls are minimal), and the insurance will be bare-bones, covering some hospital costs, for example, but not doctor visits or much preventative care. And most private insurance plans do not pay for treatment from doctors, medical labs, or hospitals that are not in their network of approved doctors or facilities.

Obamacare leaves health care in the hands of private, for-profit insurance companies, and it will do little to reduce health costs. Whether measured by the cost per person or as a percentage of total expenditures, the United States currently spends nearly twice as much on health care as does Switzerland, whose costs are second only to the United States'.

Ironically, we *already* have a kind of socialized medicine in America: Medicare. But you must be permanently disabled or over the age of sixty-five to qualify for it. Older Americans can go to almost any doctor or hospital, and the government pays the bill. It's not a perfect system, and there are holes in its coverage, but it works much the way the socialized health system works in neighboring Canada.

Does this make sense? Why do we have socialized medicine for our elderly, but not for everyone? The answer is that a lot of large corporations—hospital companies, insurance companies, drug companies, as well as many doctors and specialists—have a financial stake in the status quo. That's what we must all work hard to change.

To learn more about the fight for a humane, fair, and cost-effective national health care system in the United States, visit www.pnhp. org, the Web site of Physicians for a National Health Program, a group of thousands of health care professionals fed up with the existing system.

Chapter 18

Teach Freedom!

William Ayers

Analogy Test
Multiple Choice
High-stakes standardized testing is to learning as:
  a. *Memorizing a flight manual is to flying*
  b. *Watching* Hawaii Five-0 *is to doing police work*
  c. *Exchanging marriage vows is to a successful marriage*
  d. *Reading* Gray's Anatomy *is to practicing surgery*
  e. *Singing the national anthem is to good citizenship*
  f. *All of the above*

The typical American classroom has as much to offer an inquiring mind as does:
  a. *A vacant lot*
  b. *A mall*
  c. *A street corner*
  d. *The city dump*
  e. *The custodian's closet*
  f.   *none of the above*

The answer to each is "f"— in the first question for obvious reasons, and in the second because each of the other answers offer much more to an inquiring mind.

Capitalist Education: Into the Wreckage

Schools serve societies, and every society is reflected, for better and for worse, in its schools. Every school is both a mirror of and a window into the defining social order. If one looks at the schools hard enough, one can see the whole of the larger society; if one fully grasps the intricacies of society, one will know something about how its schools must be organized, and why.

In a totalitarian society, schools are built to teach obedience and conformity, plain and simple. In a kingdom, schools teach allegiance to the crown. An ancient agrarian community apprentices the young to become participants in a rustic world of farming. With a theocratic regime come lessons in faithfulness and piety and devotion.

These schools might be "excellent" by some standards or measures, but whatever else is taught—math or music, literature or science—the most important lessons are those that teach how to function in a specific social order. South Africa under apartheid had beautiful palaces of learning and small state-of-the-art classes for white kids—and overcrowded, dilapidated, ill-equipped classes for the African kids. That made perfect, if perverse, sense: privilege and oppression were on opposite sides of the color line, and everyone understood that hard, cruel fact. German schools in the early twentieth century produced excellent scientists, athletes, artists, and intellectuals, and they also produced submission and conformity, moral blindness, obtuse patriotism—and people for whom a pathway straight into the furnaces for some of their fellow citizens seemed acceptable.

In our capitalist society, we are insistently encouraged to think of education as a product like a car or a refrigerator, a box of bolts or a screwdriver—something bought and sold in the marketplace like any other commodity. The controlling metaphor is that the schoolhouse is a business run by a CEO: the teachers are the workers, and the students are the raw material bumping along the assembly line, getting information stuffed into their little upturned heads.

Within this model, it's easy to believe that downsizing the least productive "units" and privatizing a space that was once public is perfectly natural. It's also easy to think that teaching toward a simple standardized measurement and relentlessly applying state-administered (but privately developed and quite profitable) tests to determine the "outcomes" are a rational proxy for learning.

It's easy to think that "zero tolerance" for student misbehavior is a sane stand-in for child development or justice. And it's easy to think that centrally controlled "standards" for curriculum and teaching are commonsensical, and that "accountability"—that is, a range of sanctions on students, teachers, and schools (but never on lawmakers, foundations, corporations, or high officials) is logical and level-headed.

A merry band of billionaires, including Fortune 500 CEOs Bill Gates, Michael Bloomberg, Sam Walton, and Eli Broad, has led a wave of "school reform" within this frame—capitalist schooling on steroids. These titans spread around massive amounts of cash to promote their agenda as "common sense": dismantle public schools, crush the teachers' unions, test and punish. In other words, destroy the collective voice of teachers, sort students into winners and losers, and sell off the public square to the wealthy. This peculiar brand of schooling is part of these billionaires' social vision—that education is an individual consumer good, neither a public trust nor a social good, and certainly not a fundamental human right. It serves a society of brute competition that produces mass misery along with the iron-hard idea that such misery is the only alternative.

The education we've become accustomed to is a grotesque caricature, neither authentically nor primarily about full human development. Why, for example, is education thought of as only kindergarten through twelfth grade, or even kindergarten through university? Why does education occur only early in life? Why is there a point in our lives when we no longer think we need education? Why, again, is there a hierarchy of teacher over students? Why are there grades and grade levels? Why, indeed, do we think of a "productive" sector and a "service" sector in our society with education designated as a service activity? Why is education separate from production?

Schools for compliance and conformity are characterized by passivity and fatalism and infused with anti-intellectualism and irrelevance. They turn on the little technologies for control and normalization—the elaborate schemes for managing the mob, the knotted system of rules and discipline, the exhaustive machinery of schedules and clocks, and the laborious programs of sorting the crowd into winners and losers through testing and punishing, grading, assessing, and judging. All of this adds up to a familiar cave, an intricately constructed hierarchy—everyone in a designated place and a place for everyone. In the schools as they are here and now, knowing and accepting one's pigeonhole on the towering and barren cliff becomes the only lesson one really needs.

When the aim of education and the sole measure of success is competitive, learning becomes exclusively selfish and there is no obvious social motive to pursue it. People are turned against one another as every difference becomes a potential deficit. Getting ahead is the primary goal in such places, and mutual assistance, which can be so natural in other human affairs, is severely restricted or banned.

Beyond Capitalist Education: Trudging toward Freedom

Parents, students, citizens, teachers, and educators might press now for an education worthy of a democracy and essential to a future of free people. This would include an end to sorting people into winners and losers through standardized tests. An end to starving schools of needed resources and then blaming teachers and their unions for dismal outcomes. An end to the militarization of schools, "zero-tolerance" policies, and gender-identity discrimination. An end to the savage inequalities that deprive schools in historically segregated and poor communities of the resources they need and have rarely received. All children and youth, regardless of their economic or social circumstances, deserve full access to richly resourced classrooms led by caring, thoughtful, fully qualified, and generously compensated teachers.

The development of free people is the central goal of teaching toward and within the free society of the future. Teaching toward freedom and democracy is based on a common faith in the incalculable value of every human being and the principle that the fullest development of all is the condition for the full development of each, and, conversely, that the fullest development of each is the condition for the full development of all.

At its best, socialist education would strive for this ideal. But a hundred years of history demand that we resist lazy labels or easy assertions of political purity. We know that capitalism is an exploitative system, but socialism has often presented itself in authoritarian and narrowly nationalistic shrouds, which revolutionary humanists cannot (and should not) defend. As a teacher and an activist, I want to urge a little doubt, a hint of skepticism, a word of caution, lest we trap ourselves in the prison of a single bright and blinding idea.

Just as revolutionaries living through the death throes of feudalism could not predict with any certainty the institutions that would be born in the new age, built up within the shell of the old, we cannot do more than fight for more peace, more egalitarianism, more participation, more justice, and more democracy. We would do well to bring a strong sense of agnosticism to the effort, along with our expansive dreams of freedom, our desires, our sense of play, humor, art, surprise, and, mostly, love, which is rooted in reciprocity and always renewable. Love sharpens our senses and asks us to outdo ourselves.

In a vibrant and liberated culture, schools would make a serious commitment to free inquiry, open questioning, and full participation; access and equity and simple fairness; a curriculum that encourages independent thought and judgment. Instead of obedience and conformity, it would promote initiative, courage, imagination, and creativity.

The schools we need—and schools that we can fight for now—are lived in the present tense. The best preparation for a meaningful future life is living a meaningful present life, and so rich experiences and powerful interactions—as opposed to a bitter pill—should be on offer at schools every day. A good school or classroom is an artist's studio and a workshop for inventors, a place where experimentation with materials and investigations in the world happen every day. A good school is fearless, risk-taking, thoughtful, activist, intimate, and deep, a space where fundamental questions are pursued to their furthest limits.

Foundational questions that free people pursue might become the central stuff of our schools:

What's your story?

How is it like or unlike the stories of others?

What do we owe one another?

What does it mean to be human in the twenty-first century?

What qualities and dispositions and knowledge are of most value to humanity?

How can we nourish, develop, and organize full access to those valuable qualities?

Why are we here?

What do we want?

What kind of world could we reasonably hope to create?

How might we begin?

These questions—themes in literature and the arts through the ages—are not as lofty and distant as they might sound. In a preschool, a teacher might organize a "Me Curriculum" and interview each child, reserving a section of wall devoted to a "kid of the week" that spotlights each one, with kids telling the story of their family, how they got their first name, their favorite books and food, and more. In third grade, students might interview a "family hero" and present oral histories to the group, focused on significant events in their life, migration or movement, and life lessons learned. A group of middle-school students might spend a year exploring the environment of their neighborhood, mapping everything from housing and labor patterns to health and recreation and crime statistics.

High school kids might develop a rich and varied portfolio for graduation, a set of works to be defended in front of a committee consisting of an advisor, a peer, a teacher, a community resident, and a family member. This might consist of grades and test scores (in the short-term, as the system transitions), along with an original work of art, a physical challenge set and met, a favorite piece of writing, a record of community service, a work/study plan for the next four years, a list of the ten best books they've read, an essay on "What Makes an Educated Person," and a list of the books and essays they want to read, films they want to watch, and projects they plan to pursue in the next five years. And so on.

We learn skills, facts, and knowledge in a context. In a future free society, that context would be the pursuit of a free and productive life for all.

Our schools would resist the overspecialization of human activity, the separation of the intellectual from the manual, the head from the hand, the heart from the brain, the creative from the functional. The standard would become fluidity of function, the variation of work and capacity, the mobilization of intelligence and creativity and initiative and work in all directions.

Where active work is the order of the day, helping others is not a form of charity, something that impoverishes both the recipient and the benefactor. Rather, a spirit of open communication, interchange, and analysis becomes commonplace. In these places, there is a certain natural disorder, a certain amount of anarchy and chaos, as there is in any busy workshop. But there is a deeper discipline at work: the discipline of getting things done and learning through life.

On the side of a liberating and humanizing education lies a pedagogy of questioning, an approach that opens rather than closes the process of thinking, comparing, reasoning, perspective-taking, and dialogue. It demands something up-ending and revolutionary from students and teachers alike. Repudiate your place in the pecking order, it urges, remove that distorted, congenial mask of compliance: *You must change!*

We would learn to embrace the importance of dialogue with one another. In dialogue, one speaks with the possibility of being heard and simultaneously listens with the possibility of being changed. Dialogue is both the most hopeful and the most dangerous pedagogical practice, for in it, our own dogma and certainty and orthodoxy must be held in abeyance, must be subject to scrutiny.

The ethical core of teaching toward tomorrow must be designed to create hope and a sense of agency and possibility in students. There are three big lessons. History is still in the making, the future is unknowable, and what you do or don't do will make a difference (and, of course, choosing not to choose is itself a choice). Each of us is a work in progress—unfinished, dynamic, in-process, on the move and, yes, on the make—swimming through the wreckage toward a distant and indistinct shore. And, finally, you don't need anyone's permission to ask questions about the world.

Teachers with freedom on their minds would come to recognize that the opposite of moral is indifferent, and that the opposite of aesthetic is anesthetic. They would encourage students to become engaged participants in life, and not passive observers. They would encourage students to see the splendor and the horror, to be astonished at both the loveliness of life and all the undeserved harm and pain around us, and then to release their social imaginations in order to act on what that knowledge demands.

The challenging intellectual and ethical work of teaching pivots on our ability to see the world as it is and to see our students as three-dimensional creatures—human beings like ourselves—with hopes and dreams, aspirations, skills, and capacities; with minds and hearts and spirits; with embodied experiences, histories, and stories to tell of a past and a possible future; with families, neighborhoods, cultural surroundings, and language communities all interacting, dynamic, and entangled. This requires patience, curiosity, wonder, awe, and more than a small dose of humility. It demands sustained focus, intelligent judgment, inquiry, and investigation. It calls forth an open heart and an inquiring mind, since every judgment is contingent, every view partial, and each conclusion tentative.

In any liberating pedagogy, students become the subjects and the actors in constructing their own educations, not simply the objects of a regime of discipline and punishment. Instead of credentialing, sorting, gate-keeping, and controlling, education should enable *all* students to become smarter, more capable of negotiating our shared and complex world, better able to work effectively in and across communities to innovate and initiate with courage and creativity. This requires courage and determination—from teachers, families, communities, and students—to build alternative and insurgent classrooms and schools and community spaces focused on what we know we need rather than what we are told we must endure. We must transform education from rote boredom and endlessly alienating routines into something that is eye-popping and mind-blowing—always opening doors and opening minds and opening hearts as students forge their own pathways into an expansive world.

Knowledge is an inherently *public* good, something that can be reproduced at little or no cost. Like love, it's generative: the more you have, the better off you become; the more you give away, the more you have. Offering knowledge and learning and education to others diminishes nothing. In a flourishing democracy, knowledge would be shared without any reservation or restrictions whatsoever. This points us toward an education that could be about full human development, enlightenment, and freedom.

Chapter 19

Imagining Art After Capitalism

Mat Callahan

What will art and art-making become once capitalism is a thing of the past? The end of corporate tyranny will be the end of the music, film, publishing, and telecommunications industries as well as the Ford, Rockefeller, Mellon, and other foundations that combine to dominate art production, distribution, and consumption today. Emancipated from the rigid hierarchies and mental slavery these institutions have imposed, art and art-making will enjoy a renaissance. Not only will there be an abundance of works celebrating a new world being born, but there will be unprecedented creative expression inspiring new conceptions of what art and art-making consist of. This will surely lead to novel forms and practices that are difficult to predict. But it is possible to trace certain outlines and imagine some of the challenges and opportunities that lie ahead. In any case, it won't be Disneyland.

People aroused and mobilized to carry out society's renewal will view fundamental questions in a new light. Among these will undoubtedly be the question of ownership. When it comes to land, water, air, and the production necessary to society's material well-being, there may be a wide range of proposals for what best serves the common good. But one thing is clear: the ownership of ideas will be exposed as a sham and a delusion. It follows that the elaborate fiction of intellectual property will simply be abolished. Owning ideas is impossible; the regimes of copyright, patent, and trademark have been enshrined in law and in popular consciousness to the detriment of creativity and the sharing of the infinite bounty of the human imagination. Since artists will no longer need to fear being ripped off, able instead to count on credit and remuneration for their effort, the dubious protections copyright provides will serve no purpose. At a stroke such impediments to freedom would be done away with, and the problems and promise they have so long obscured will become immediately apparent.

Society will commit its resources to the making of art—not only the costs of materials or instruments but also of the maintenance of artists, whose training, skill, and talent combine to make them specialists. Publishers, record companies, promoters, and publicists will no longer be needed, since they serve only one purpose: the private accumulation of wealth. Necessary tasks such as editing, curating, and art criticism will be liberated from servility to financial gain. Instead of guarding formulaic mediocrity to ensure profitability, critical evaluation will be dedicated to serving art and society.

Credit for the contributions individuals make will be given freely when credit is no longer constrained by who is getting paid, who owns the work, or who is the most famous, ruthless, or conniving. Indeed, credit will be more accurately and fairly assigned to all those contributing to a work and not only the "lone genius" who rarely, if ever, is solely responsible for any work of art.

This is not to underestimate the individual or the solitude required for much creative work. On the contrary, freed from the cutthroat competition for status and rank, the individual artist could acknowledge influences, artistic peers, and audience without fearing the diminishment of his or her own gifts. Indeed, sharing is a basic motive for art-making, and sharing one's gifts will become commonplace and be allowed to flourish. Simultaneously, the value of art will cease to be economic—money will no longer be the motive or criteria for making art—and its aesthetic, educational, and imaginative value will be restored to preeminence. Purged of the pecuniary, art and art-making will valorize themselves and the world to which they contribute, and not the bourgeois patron, demagogic politician, or the egotism and glorification of the privileged. Indeed, art may eventually cease to be a separate and distinct category and instead be woven into the fabric of social life: not only might everyone join in, but the beautiful and imaginative might become the purpose of what anyone does.

Such vistas will clarify, indeed demystify, another crucial distinction: that between the education of artists and the uses of art in the education of all. Consider the education of artists, and questions of freedom of expression, allocation of resources, and the criteria by which art is judged arise, reminding us that these are not questions created by capitalism alone. Indeed, they are questions that arose with the stratification of society and the specialization that corresponded to changing modes of production long before capitalism triumphed. Surpassing capitalism does not, therefore, mean an end to conflict; it is, in fact, more likely that conflict will increase. But its character will be different, as will the means of its resolution. In a society promoting the public interest and maximizing equality, particularly in relation to the allocation of resources and the health and welfare of all its members, conflict need no longer carry with it the threat of death, imprisonment, or impoverishment. Debate will be encouraged, particularly in the realm of ideas, especially in the arts and sciences. There will no doubt be heated argument over who decides which artists or projects get public support. There will likely be endless discussion over what is the good, the beautiful, and the true, and what is only a matter of taste. But for once, the question of mastery—not the mastery of slaves but the mastery of a craft—would gain its proper place in both the training of artists and the judgment of art.

In the case of education in general, the purpose must be to liberate the imagination, elevate the aspirations, and bring about a radical change in the way human beings collaborate with each other and with their environment. Furthering this process requires expanding the role of the arts in educating children. It has been proven over and over, even within capitalism, that art in education is crucial to the formation of critically thinking people. Using art in education militates against the production of the psychopathic personality so common under capitalism. What gives art in education its specific role is precisely that it encourages the free expression of creativity—not for material reward, but for the joy and illumination of creativity itself. This will, of course, lead to learning more, learning better, and achieving specific goals with material benefit. But the basis for the success of art in education resides in the very processes of art-making, what is necessary to artists and how they enlighten and inspire the student.

Two aspects of art-making distinguish it from politics. First, art-making is not necessarily democratic. Even if democracy or the common good is extolled in a work of art, the process of making it requires discipline and dedication to a craft, not to the decisions of an elected group or representative assembly. Even if there are no more gods or masters, there are the physical and imaginative materials with which artists work that will speak and direct them: the paint, stone, film images, musical instruments, words, or sound, and the ideas, dreams, and visions that arise in the mind. While artists may employ cooperative effort and democratic decision-making, that is only one of many ways art can be made—and not necessarily the best or ideal way, as it might be in politics.

Second, art has diverse functions, from decorative to educational to spiritual. Art cannot be narrowly defined or confined to one or another function, least of all to being solely for entertainment or diversion. The result of centuries of commerce in art has been the erection of barriers and the fostering of antagonism among artists competing for resources and recognition. It has pitted professional artists, professional art critics, gallery owners, museum curators, concert promoters, and music, film, and theatrical producers against the general public. The simple fact is that throughout history the populace has produced its own art. The common people do not need anyone to make art for them, and certainly not for an elite corps of pampered parasites. One need only recall the music of African slaves and their descendants to know that virtuosity, emotional depth, and imaginative insight are abundant in popular art and were in fact expropriated to enrich a few at the expense of the many. In the course of a revolutionary social transformation, however, the relations between artists and the general public would necessarily change from one where stars and celebrities parade their precious gifts before an adoring herd of onlookers to one where free people would be the judges of artistic quality and defenders of expression unfettered by financial or selfish interest. After all, if ordinary people are deciding how best to allocate the resources they have themselves produced, to whom would artists appeal for support? There would undoubtedly be intense argument, but it would no longer involve the corporate bean counter, studio mogul, or wealthy patron to whom the artist has to bow, beg, and plead. Rather, requests would likely be made to committees or community groups assigned the responsibility of encouraging the development of art in the public interest.

Such committees might include trained artists, educators, and members of the community with no special training. They would shift the focus of art production from the Hollywood model of big-budget spectacles made for global consumption to the production of art on a local and regional basis. Not only will this return to the local community the authority to decide what it wants to make and to share, it also would encourage art to draw on the rich variety of particular experience that has been systematically excluded by the standardized formulas best suited for mass consumption. Finally, the consultative process would necessarily be ongoing and integrated into both art-making in its own right and into arts in education, thus encouraging greater appreciation of art history and the development of artistic skill by everyone. This does not preclude the widespread, even global appeal of certain works or artists. But it does shift the emphasis from top-down decision-making and centralized production and distribution to what can be made and controlled by local and regional communities.

Earlier attempts at revolution and socialism reveal sharp contradictions between the arts, the sciences, and politics that cannot be overlooked. Art educates. Not in the same way that mathematics or astronomy or geology educates, but it teaches nonetheless. This didactic function brings with it a challenge to political and scientific authority because the way art "knows" is by way of the imagination and not necessarily by way of reason. The material that imagination uses to produce its results may exist only in the mind of the imaginer. The material that reason uses and the results thereby produced begin with what already exists outside the mind of the reasoner. Both require thought, but the imaginary need only captivate the imagination to be real, while reason requires logical or empirical evidence to substantiate itself. The clash that results can be creative or destructive, depending on how well the contradictions are handled. If scientific method and popular unity are strong, then there is nothing to fear from the wildest flights of the imagination. Artistic freedom—including the responsibility to struggle over art's social effects—is in fact an important measure of the health of any society, especially a socialist one. But once the culture industry is no more, once the creation of "stars" and "hits" is a thing of the past, then the illusions these institutions have been constructed to create will also be made a thing of the past. More importantly, these illusions will be desacralized, and instead of people worshipping at the shrine of a dead Elvis or a living Madonna, they will be free to marvel at the infinite universe and their own creative expression within it.

In building new institutions or structures for the making of art, the fundamental connection between artist and community will be made explicit rather than draped in the mystique or unthinking worship of the divine origin of talent. There can be no doubt that there are mysteries and wonders that lie at the very heart of art-making. There can be no doubt that some artists are unusually gifted with skills and insight we can only marvel at. But such gifts and talents can be celebrated as part of our common human heritage and not the sole possession of a dominant class anointed by God or Mammon. In practical terms this will likely mean that a very small number of artists who are firmly allied with capitalism and thoroughly imbued with a dominator ideology will suffer ignominy and defeat. But this is what revolution necessarily entails. Defenders of the old are forcibly removed and the new is born from ashes. This historical fact must not be allowed to obscure the principle that the minimization of suffering and injustice will be enjoyed by the great majority, and to serve the people will be an inspiring opportunity, not an oppressive duty.

Fundamentally, art is an activity—not an object fixed in canvas, stone, tape, or computer file. Art is something people do, and then there is an end to that activity. That end is often, but not always, a finished work. As a finished work, however, art's principal purpose is to reinvigorate the process of art-making—in other words, to begin again the activity that is its foundation. Of all the destructive and repressive effects of commerce in art and capitalism in general, perhaps the most egregious is the denigration of labor, activity, participation, and ultimately life itself. Capitalism's purpose is to hoard limitless quantities of dead objects, especially artwork, by which rank, prestige, and, ultimately, power can be measured. The pious pontificating of art critics and pop music journalists perpetuate a great hoax for which many artists have paid the price: if your art doesn't sell, you're no good. People make art because they love to make it. Buying and selling have nothing to do with this. Indeed, what separates art from the making of other things is that it does not need a purpose or use other than the joy it brings and the insight it provides. It is nevertheless a component of human existence without which we would be no different than other animals.

The great freedom that awaits artists after the demise of capitalism is that the magic they weave, the illusions they spin, the mysteries they conjure, the spirits they unleash will not be fakery, snake oil, or deception. Art will no longer be forced to conspire with its own enslavement. What will matter most will be the process by which art-making informs and inspires human being and the collective effort for the common good. As both haven of the timeless and herald of the new, art will sing the birth of humanity.

Chapter 20

Prometheus Completely Unbound: What Science and Technology Could Accomplish in a Socialist America

Clifford D. Conner

The Greek Prometheus myth has often been invoked as a metaphor for the inhibition of scientific and technological progress by social forces hostile to change. The myth credited the demigod Prometheus with empowering the human race by teaching us astronomy, mathematics, architecture, navigation, metallurgy, and medicine. That greatly upset the god-in-chief, Zeus, who had wanted us mere mortals to remain stupid, docile, and no threat to his power. As punishment, Zeus had Prometheus chained to a pillar in the Caucasus Mountains and left him there for a long, long time.

Human creativity could never be entirely squelched, but progress in science and technology throughout most of human history has been held back by traditional cultures in which the abundance of slave and serf labor gave no incentive for inventing "labor-saving" devices. Like Zeus, the ruling classes of those societies often discouraged scientific creativity because they feared its socially disruptive consequences. (The best-known example in the West is the persecution of Galileo for championing the view that the Earth revolves around the Sun.) The rise of capitalism in early modern Europe, however, brought forth a new social system that at first strongly encouraged innovation and invention.

In the late eighteenth and the nineteenth centuries, an unprecedented burst of technological progress known as the Industrial Revolution transformed the world. Historians have called it the era of "Prometheus Unbound." And from the steam engine to the iPad, the parade of innovations has been spectacular. Airplanes! Television! Computers! Space exploration! If there is one way in which Homo sapiens can be said to have made progress over the past two centuries, it would seem to be in the conjoined areas of science and technology.

At the beginning of the capitalist epoch, the competition between small producers spurred creativity and innovation, but now a handful of "too big to fail" conglomerates dominate the economy, which tends to stifle that competition. The production-for-profit system has forged new chains for Prometheus—or at least put him under house arrest. Rather than being free to benefit the human race as a whole, science and technology have been forced to serve the private interests of giant corporations.

From its origins in the Industrial Revolution, the progress that the profit motive stimulated was directed toward enriching an economic elite—the owners of capital. New inventions and techniques were promoted as labor-saving devices. But in practice, these innovations did not decrease laborers' working hours or lighten their burden in any way. Instead, they gave manufacturers the ability to turn out more products with fewer workers, which meant that a major consequence of technological advances was layoffs. These inventions would be more accurately described as "labor *cost* saving," because they have primarily benefited the factory owners by decreasing their payrolls.

Planned obsolescence is another way the profit motive distorts technological progress. Rather than applying their ingenuity to creating things that resist deterioration, researchers have often been paid to do the opposite: to design products to wear out so that consumers will be compelled to replace them sooner. Reorienting researchers toward *improving* consumer goods—toward building them to last—would go a long way in freeing Prometheus from his chains.

Among the most familiar examples of the way corporate dominance of research has afflicted science and technology is Big Pharma—the monopolization of medicines and research on medicines by a handful of multinational pharmaceutical manufacturers. The fruits of Big Pharma's laboratories are treated as business secrets, which violates a basic principle of good science: that knowledge advances when it is freely exchanged. Because Big Pharma's primary concern is profit, it would rather develop drugs for relatively minor conditions that affluent people must take regularly for years than work on medicines to treat diseases that mainly afflict poor people, such as malaria. Also, if research indicates that its drugs might be ineffective or dangerous, it often sweeps those results under the rug.

Science for War

In the United States since World War II, the corporations have joined together with university laboratories and government agencies to form a single entity known as Big Science. The main source of Big Science's research funding has been the federal military budget. Much other science spending has been war research in disguise. The US space program, for example, was largely motivated by its potential military applications.

Big Science began with the Manhattan Project, which created the means to vaporize the human population of two Japanese cities. During the Cold War, massive military spending fed the growth of the military-industrial complex, the web of the Pentagon and large corporations such as aircraft and electronics manufacturers that built its ever more sophisticated weaponry. This did not change after the Cold War ended. The American economy has become hopelessly addicted to war spending.

As a result, science and technology in the United States have been firmly oriented toward destructive and antihuman ends. Some of it is patently useless, such as the billions of dollars spent on the Reagan administration's Strategic Defense Initiative, popularly known as Star Wars—a wacky notion that a shield could be constructed in outer space to protect the United States from incoming missiles.

Yet the weapons that *do* work are a bigger and more destructive waste. From nuclear weapons to the development of remote-control war, wherein drone aircraft operated from computers in Iowa rain death and destruction on rural Pakistan, a huge part of the United States' scientific endeavors in the past seventy years has been devoted to finding more effective ways to kill people.

Spitting Into the Well We Drink From

There is one major area in which the consequences could be even more dire than those of war. The reckless growth of industrial production has damaged the environment in ways that threaten the existence of the human race, if not all life on Earth. It pumps tons of poisons into the air we breathe, the water we drink, and the soil in which our food is grown.

It seems utterly irrational that a society would spit into the well from which it drinks, but the decision-making process that allows it to happen is controlled by corporate interests rather than by the society as a whole.

Two of the most environmentally destructive energy technologies are legally shielded from paying the costs of the damages they cause: fracking and nuclear power. Fracking—shorthand for hydraulic fracturing—is a technological marvel, a way to extract natural gas from deep underground by injecting fluid under high pressure to break up the rock layers that contain the gas. The toxic fluids used in the process poison underground sources of drinking water. But the private corporations that extract the gas don't have to pay for the increased medical costs, illnesses, and deaths caused by polluted water.

Nuclear power plants, even when they operate "safely"—that is, if they don't have spectacular accidents like Chernobyl in 1986 or Fukushima in 2011—release radioactivity that causes cancer and birth defects into the Earth's atmosphere and waters. Yet the American government still promotes nuclear power, props up the industry artificially with huge subsidies, and limits its liability from lawsuits if a major accident occurs.

Big Oil and its political allies have paralyzed efforts to confront the threat of global warming, whether by reducing carbon dioxide emissions or by developing alternative technologies—especially the conversion of solar energy to electricity. They finance think tanks that produce pseudoscientific reports denying climate change, and they fund the campaigns of legislators who defend their interests.

Can Science and Technology Thrive Without the Profit Motive?

It is often alleged that the creativity necessary to advance science and technology cannot exist without the monetary incentives provided by the free-market economic system. But the experiences of the Soviet Union, China, and Cuba reveal that science and technology can not only exist without capitalist incentives, they can thrive.

The Soviet Union transformed itself from a scientific backwater to a great power in the world of science within a few decades. In 1957, it became the first country to launch an artificial satellite, and in 1961, it became the first to put an astronaut into orbit. Its success derived from the ability of a centralized economy to marshal and organize resources.

The Soviet Union's large-scale technological feats—hydroelectric power plants, nuclear weapons, earth-orbiting satellites, and the like—were spectacular. But in spite of all that, its record was ultimately disappointing. Given the immense size of the Soviet science establishment, its achievements fell short of what might have been expected of it.

China's experience was similar. In 1949, the Chinese Revolution brought to power a government that, despite the country's poverty, had the will and the ability to create institutions of Big Science. The Soviet Union provided more than a model. In the 1950s, Soviet scientists and technicians participated heavily in the construction of science in the new China, and they created it in their own image.

But in 1960, the Soviet Union abruptly withdrew its support. Thousands of Soviet scientists and engineers were called home immediately, taking their blueprints and expertise with them. In spite of this devastating blow, China accomplished some remarkable achievements in nuclear and space technology—another testament to the power of a planned economy to mobilize and focus resources. The country tested its first atomic bomb in 1964 and its first hydrogen bomb in 1967, and it launched its first satellite into Earth orbit in 1970. In 2003, it became one of only three nations to launch an astronaut into space.

The Chinese science establishment, however, remained highly bureaucratized and focused on military and big industrial projects at the expense of research aimed at improving the lives of the nation's billion-plus people. Most Chinese endure a standard of living far below that of the people of Europe, Japan, and the United States.

That an orientation more centered on human needs is possible has been demonstrated by the revolution that occurred in 1959 in a much smaller country: Cuba. Once the leaders of the Cuban Revolution were in command of a fully nationalized economy, they enjoyed the same advantages that had enabled their Soviet and Chinese counterparts to develop powerful science establishments. Cuba, however, is an island with only about ten million people. There was no way it could compete with the United States in the field of military technology. Instead, Cuba would depend on diplomatic and political means for its national security—that is, on its alliance with the Soviet Union and on the moral authority its revolution had gained throughout Latin America and the rest of the world. That allowed its science establishment to focus its work on other fields.

The USSR and China had both sought to build powerful, autonomous economies that could compete head to head with the world's leading capitalist nations. They aimed their science efforts at facilitating the growth of basic heavy industry. The Cubans, by contrast, oriented their science program toward solving social problems. Universal health care was assigned top priority, and it became more important when the harsh economic embargo imposed by the United States compelled the Cubans to find ways to produce their own medicines. They met the challenge. The upshot was that Cuba, despite its "developing world" economic status, now stands at the forefront of international biochemical and pharmacological research.

In the 1980s, a worldwide biotechnological revolution occurred, and Cuban research institutions took a leading role. Among the most noteworthy products of Cuban bioscience are vaccines for treating meningitis and hepatitis B, the popular cholesterol-reducer PPG (which is derived from sugarcane), monoclonal antibodies used to combat the rejection of transplanted organs, recombinant interferon products for use against viral infections, epidermal growth factor to promote tissue healing in burn victims, and recombinant streptokinase for treating heart disease.

The Cuban biotech institutes focus their attention on deadly diseases that Big Pharma tends to ignore because they mainly afflict poor people in poor countries. An important part of their mission is the creation of low-cost alternative drugs. In 2003, Cuban researchers announced the invention of the world's first human vaccine containing a synthetic antigen (the "active ingredient" of a vaccine). It was a vaccine for preventing Hib (Haemophilus influenzae type b), a bacterial disease that causes meningitis and pneumonia in young children and kills more than five hundred thousand people throughout the world every year. An effective vaccine against Hib had already been proven successful in industrialized nations, but its high cost sharply limited its availability in the less affluent countries.

The Cuban revolution's scientific achievements testify that important, high-level scientific work can be performed without being driven by the profit motive. They also show that centralized planning does not necessarily have to follow the ultra-bureaucratic model offered by the Soviet Union and China, where science was used more to strengthen the state than to meet the needs of the people. Cuba's accomplishments are all the more impressive because it has a relatively small economic base and has also been handicapped by a US economic embargo that has prevented the importation of medicines, medical technology, and even routine medical supplies. A 2010 Amnesty International report concluded that despite Cuba's advances in the medical field, the US blockade has endangered the health of millions of Cubans.

The Cuban experience has come closest to demonstrating the possibility of a fully human-oriented science. Although Cuba's small size limits its usefulness as a basis for comparison, its accomplishments in the medical sciences certainly prove that science on a global scale could be redirected from its present course as a facilitator of military power and blind economic growth and instead be devoted to improving the well-being of entire populations.

Removing the Roadblock to Genuine Progress

Even with Prometheus under house arrest by the American war machine, many technological marvels have been produced. But their primary purpose has not been to improve the human condition. The innovations that have been beneficial, such as radar and the Internet, have for the most part been by-products of military research.

The change in priorities accompanying a socialist transformation of America would redirect an immense amount of scientific talent and resources toward conquering hunger, poverty, and disease throughout the world. Socialized research and development—democratically controlled and centrally planned—would remove the obstacles that private interests have placed in the way of the free development of science. Who can imagine, for example, what medical science might accomplish if liberated from the clutches of Big Pharma and the financial predators of the insurance industry?

In a society geared toward serving human needs, labor-saving technology would not lead to workers losing their jobs but to reducing their working hours without a reduction in pay. And by not ignoring the social costs of technological progress instead of greasing the slippery slope to environmental destruction, new technology could actually help pull us out of the mess capitalism has created.

Free Prometheus now!

Chapter 21

First-Class News:
The Media in a Socialist USA

Fred Jerome

Imagine a world without the *New York Times*, Fox News, CNN, the *Wall Street Journal*, and countless other tools used by the 1 percent to rule and fool.

In a socialist society run by and for the working people it represents, the mega-monopolies like Walmart, Halliburton, Exxon-Mobil, and the corporations that run the tightly controlled "mainstream media" will be a thing of the past.

It's not news that the major US media are run by and for big business, or that the major media companies are themselves big businesses. Twenty years ago, thirty corporations controlled 90 percent of US media. Today, it is a grand total of six mega-corporations—Rupert Murdoch's News Corporation, Disney, Viacom, Time Warner, CBS, and Comcast. Besides accumulating their own profits, the media are daily trumpets for the rest of the corporate world's advertising.

If you've ever worked for a newspaper or magazine, you know the process of layout and design. The ads are laid out before anything else except the lead stories; the other news and feature stories are then fit between ads. "What can we find to fill this hole?" an editor will frequently shout, referring to a page where stories have not yet been designated to fill the space between the ads, thus leaving a "news hole." Media owners' profits do not come primarily from the money we spend to buy their publications, but from the ads inside them. While big advertisers don't directly select what news is published, publishers, editors, and news directors know what they like and will rarely risk their disapproval.

"It would be foolish to expect objective reporting: not because journalists are bad people, but because of the economic structure of the organizations they work for," Arundhati Roy wrote in 2011. "In fact, what is surprising is that despite all this, occasionally there is some very good reporting. But overall we have silence, or a completely distorted picture."

Online news sources also rely on ads for their profits even more than their print-media cousins. So do the search engines and portal sites through which people gain access to them, such as Google and Yahoo!. But it's online media that have the potential for wider than ever public participation and exchange of views.

A democratic, accessible-to-all media will move to center stage in a socialist USA. In some ways this democratization of the media is already happening on the Internet. But the government's ability to spy on and even turn off the Internet belies any real democracy. In a socialist democracy, working people will control the political process, the way in which they make a living, and collectively and individually, they will influence mass culture. The Internet will be a powerful and democratizing tool in this effort.

Yet the media business, for those who now own and run it, is more than just a money-making operation. The owners also promote their political agenda. Through selecting and disseminating news—or presenting propaganda like "the recession is over" or "drones almost always hit their targets"—the media moguls push the public to support that agenda, from their political candidates to their wars. In capitalist societies, what's reported as "news" is selected, organized, and presented by an army of self-important publishers, editors, and writers who—if they want to keep their jobs—follow their corporate employers' political line. And what's *not* reported is often just as telling. In 2012, Fairness and Accuracy in Reporting noted that less than one percent of news stories in eight major outlets covered poverty.

Indeed, almost a century ago, Upton Sinclair, in *The Brass Check*, defined journalism in the United States as "the day-to-day, between-elections propaganda, whereby the minds of the people are kept in a state of acquiescence, so that when the crisis of an election comes, they go to the polls and cast their ballots for either one of the two candidates of their exploiters."

But what will the media be like in a socialist USA? There is no blueprint, but in a society that has erased corporate control, the articles in newspapers and magazines and online will not be filler between ads for teeth whiteners and weight-loss pills. There won't be TV commercials for Coke, cars, or million-dollar condos. There will be no private corporations to create and sponsor the news.

Most of us could probably manage to struggle through life without Coca-Cola and Colgate, but who, then, will pay for the news? Who will pay the salaries of reporters, camera people, technicians, announcers, maintenance staff, online journalists, professional bloggers, and videographers?

In a socialist society a portion of the media would be reserved for news disseminated by the democratically elected governing bodies, that is, working people elected by and for working people. But state ownership is not the only way media can represent the interests of working people, to speak with or through their voices. In most cases, the media would be owned and operated by working-class organizations—labor unions, neighborhood associations, and cultural centers.

So news (and views) in a socialist society will be brought to you by a plethora of noncommercial sponsors. The government media will report on and discuss, for example, the major government plans for production, how to improve education, and more. But other media—newspapers, TV and radio stations, and Web sites sponsored by workers' organizations, cultural organizations, youth groups, sports teams, and neighborhood groups will report on issues specific to their interests.

Socialist media will be multisponsored and multifaceted and reflect a range of opinions even when there are disagreements and arguments.

But what about the cost? Can workers' organizations such as labor unions, tenants' organizations, or citywide parent-teacher associations really afford to pay for daily and weekly newspapers, magazines, TV and radio newscasts, blogs, and online audio- and video-streaming techniques?

In most cases, workers could meet the cost of media-making with add-ons to union dues, but that may not always be needed. New technology has drastically cut the costs of producing media. Smaller, easier-to-use cameras, recorders, and other airwave technology, as well as the electronic publication of books, newsletters, and blogs, have brought media production within the reach of almost everyone.

Union dues today pay for the publication, including staff salaries, of many union newspapers. In a socialist society, where money is allocated based on assessed social need and not on projected profits, government will subsidize many salaries in social, economic, political, and educational areas. (Even under capitalism, the government funds public schools, although usually in a distorted manner through which schools in wealthier areas get the most money.) So salaries at the media operations of smaller unions will most likely be covered by government subsidies.

The organizational outreach of such workers' groups—through their affiliates and friends across the country (and often around the world) will provide the circulation that is so critical—and in capitalist society, so costly.

But what about bias? Can a newspaper or TV news program run by the autoworkers' union, for example, provide critical reports about that union's problems and weaknesses? When workers on one section of an auto assembly line feel that the line is moving too fast for safety—perhaps it has already caused some minor injuries, and they believe a major accident is inevitable—while union officials are publicly boasting about their plant's speed and "socialist efficiency," will the union's TV program invite the complaining workers on the air to discuss their issues? Indeed, will *Autoworkers News and Views* on TV have a regular segment devoted to union members' criticisms?

Why not? Who better to discuss and debate problems inside a union than the members who live with and often suffer from those problems? If unions or neighborhood councils are truly trying to make things better for their members, what more effective tools than media outlets to spur such improvements?

But the main difference between news media under socialism and the news media we know today will be what gets covered. Since the first hieroglyphics, the role of the media has been to spread the word—to disseminate news (and views) to readers, listeners, and viewers. And from the very beginning, the number-one question has been: Whose news and whose views?

With no corporate padlocks, the media door will be open for a variety of forms different from the news we're permitted today. Instead of assigning reporters and editors to cover beats (and often it's not just beats but entire sections of each day's news) such as celebrity weddings or Wall Street wheeling and dealing, socialist media will have beats of a different class—working-class beats. Instead of who makes profit—and how much profit—from the sale of GM trucks, socialist media will cover who makes those trucks. They would also talk to the people who drive those trucks, to evaluate their safety features and propose new ones.

Imagine the news media with no Wall Street business reports, no stock-market prices—the socialist economy will no longer be controlled by Wall Street businesses. Indeed, there will be no big businesses on Wall (or any other) Street, and no stock market. News media will no longer report on the president's golf game or the first lady's new dress, or propagandize for war, or lie about and cover up scandals.

To be sure, there will be no shortage of economic news in a socialist society. Some news will still come from local and national governments that set product-distribution quotas or help to negotiate them, sponsor trade and international exchange with other countries, and—if the world is still partly controlled by capitalist powers—organize defense against economic (as well as cultural, and possibly military) assaults. But most news reports in socialist media will come from working people themselves. Here are a few news-story possibilities:

- At an air-conditioner factory in Brooklyn, a man and a woman on the assembly line recently both lost a finger in an accident in the grid-cutting operation. When the workers first tried using safety gloves to protect their hands, they were so bulky that it was almost impossible to operate the machinery effectively. They came up with a thinner glove, which was better for working but not strong enough to prevent blades from slicing through. Finally, with help from their machinists union local, several plant workers developed, tested, and installed a new electric-eye "hand shield" that automatically shuts down the line before any injury can occur. This might well be a national news story, especially if there was controversy over whether the new device shut down the line unnecessarily and thereby impaired production.

- A union theater group, part of the nationwide New Workers Theater League that is often in the culture section of the media, produces new dramas written by workers as well as old but still popular pieces like *Threepenny Opera*, *Waiting for Lefty*, and *West Side Story*.

- There could also be reports of school poetry slams, neighborhood art shows, music festivals, rival baseball teams, cooking contests, and dance parties.

And there will be stories of continuing struggles to make sure that the revolution represents the entire working class—especially struggles against the old but adhesive attitudes of racism and sexism. In a society where racism and sexism are as widespread as they are in the United States, they will not evaporate simply because revolutionaries nail a "closed" sign to the door of the New York Stock Exchange.

Discussions, debates, even battles will continue, and social justice committees will be elected by the union membership to look into complaints and to dig up and root out capitalist, racist, and sexist weeds that continue to grow.

Social justice committees in each workplace and community will have no shortage of complaints to consider—and the media will have no shortage of stories to investigate.

Besides reporting news, the media will be key to ensuring the fullest public discussion and debate of policies under consideration by national and local governments, as well as of proposed changes in local workplaces, schools, and communities. Functioning as a public forum in this way will involve more than simply letters to the editor and interviews with readers.

Online media will continue to play its vital role. Social media platforms such as Facebook, Twitter, and blogs strengthen discussion and debate and ensure that all readers have a voice in the societal dialogue.

Moreover, working people, students of all ages, and retired people, all can and will also launch their own reports and discussions, only adding to the sense of participatory democracy. The major news media—municipal, regional, or national—can and almost certainly will include selections of highlights from local online forum discussions and blogs.

These media forums will also include sections—perhaps certain pages, perhaps certain days of the week—for discussion and debate about readers' everyday problems. Children, teenagers, and young adults would have their own columns.

There will be many other features in the media of a socialist society. One would certainly be "never forget," stories in words and pictures—on-air or online or both—describing battles waged previously during life under capitalism: tent cities for homeless families, "stop-and-frisk" police policies that singled out young black and Latino men, and the experience of unemployment and long-term joblessness. But "Never Forget" would also feature stories about fighting capitalist oppression through strikes and marches, and about heroes of past struggles.

Besides "Never Forget" columns in the daily and weekly media, a series of historical TV specials or mini-magazines on themes such as the Native American resistance movement, labor organizing, and the fight against racism could be produced by student journalists working with older folks who took part in those struggles. These would also be available to teachers for classroom use.

Stories about life under capitalism, about the struggles to create a new and just society, and about forming a socialist democracy will all make for compelling reading. It is up to us to make sure this happens.

GETTING THERE: HOW TO MAKE A SOCIALIST AMERICA

Chapter 22

Where Does Occupy Wall Street Go from Here? A Proposal

Michael Moore

The following originally appeared on MichaelMoore.com on Nov. 22, 2011.

Friends, this past weekend I participated in a four-hour meeting of Occupy Wall Street activists whose job it is to come up with the vision and goals of the movement. It was attended by more than forty people, and the discussion was both inspiring and invigorating. Here is what we ended up proposing as the movement's "vision statement" to the General Assembly of Occupy Wall Street:

We Envision:

1. a truly free, democratic and just society;
2. where we, the people, come together and solve our problems by consensus;
3. where people are encouraged to take personal and collective responsibility and participate in decision-making;
4. where we learn to live in harmony and embrace principles

of toleration and respect for diversity and the differing views of others;

5. where we secure the civil and human rights of all from violation by tyrannical forces and unjust governments;

6. where political and economic institutions work to benefit all, not just the privileged few;

7. where we provide full and free education to everyone, not merely to get jobs but to grow and flourish as human beings;

8. where we value human needs over monetary gain, to ensure decent standards of living without which effective democracy is impossible;

9. where we work together to protect the global environment to ensure that future generations will have safe and clean air, water, and food supplies, and will be able to enjoy the beauty and bounty of nature that past generations have enjoyed.

The next step will be to develop a specific list of goals and demands. As one of the millions of people who are participating in the Occupy Wall Street movement, I would like to respectfully offer my suggestions for what we can all get behind *now* to wrestle the control of our country out of the hands of the 1 percent and place it squarely with the 99 percent majority.

Here is what I will propose to the General Assembly of Occupy Wall Street:

Ten Things We Want

1. Eradicate the Bush tax cuts for the rich and institute new taxes on the wealthiest Americans and on corporations, including a tax on all trading on Wall Street (where they currently pay nothing).

2. Assess a penalty tax on any corporation that moves American jobs to other countries when that company is already making profits in America. Our jobs are the most important national treasure, and they cannot be removed from the country simply because someone wants to make more money.

3. Require that *all* Americans pay the same Social Security tax on *all* of their earnings. Normally, working people pay about 6 percent of their income to Social Security, but someone making $1 million a year pays about 0.6 percent of theirs. This law would simply make the rich pay what everyone else pays.

4. Reinstate the Glass-Steagall Act, placing serious regulations on how business is conducted by Wall Street and the banks.

5. Investigate the Crash of 2008, and bring to justice those who committed any crimes.

6. Reorder our nation's spending priorities. Ending of all foreign wars would save their cost of over $2 billion a week. We'd use this money to reopen libraries, reinstate band and art and civics classes in our schools, fix our roads and bridges and infrastructure, wire the entire country for twenty-first-century Internet, and support scientific research that improves our lives.

7. Join the rest of the free world and create a single-payer, free, and universal health-care system that covers all Americans all of the time.

8. Immediately reduce carbon emissions that are destroying the planet and discover ways to live without the oil that will be depleted and gone by the end of the century.

9. Require corporations with more than 10,000 employees to restructure their board of directors so that 50 percent of its members are elected by the company's workers. We can

never have a real democracy as long as most people have no say in what happens at the place they spend most of their time: their job. (For any US businesspeople freaking out at this idea because you think workers can't run a successful company: Germany has a law like this, and it has helped to make Germany the world's leading manufacturing exporter.)

10. We, the people, must pass three constitutional amendments that will go a long way toward fixing the core problems we now have. These include:

1. Fixing our broken electoral system by
   a. completely removing campaign contributions from the political process;
   b. requiring all elections to be publicly financed;
   c. moving Election Day to the weekend to increase voter turnout;
   d. making all Americans registered voters at the moment of their birth; and
   e. banning computerized voting and requiring that all elections take place on paper ballots.
2. Declaring that corporations are not people and do not have the constitutional rights of citizens. This amendment should also state that the interests of the general public and society must always come before the interests of corporations.
3. A second Bill of Rights as proposed by President Franklin D. Roosevelt: That every American has a human right to employment, to health care, and a free and full education; to breathe clean air, drink clean water, and eat safe food; and to be cared for with dignity and respect in their old age.

Let me know what you think. Occupy Wall Street enjoys the support of millions. It is a movement that cannot be stopped. Become part of it by sharing your thoughts with me or online at occupywallst.org.

Get involved in (or start) your own local Occupy movement: howtooccupy.org.

Make some noise. You don't have to pitch a tent in lower Manhattan to be an Occupier. You are one just by saying you are. This movement has no singular leader or spokesperson. Every participant is a leader in their neighborhood, their school, their place of work. Each of you is a spokesperson to those whom you encounter. There are no dues to pay, no permission to seek in order to create an action.

We are but ten weeks old, yet we have already changed the national conversation. This is our moment, the one we've been hoping for, waiting for. If it's going to happen, it has to happen now. Don't sit this one out. This is the real deal. This is it.

Chapter 23

What I Would Do as Attorney General

Michael Ratner

It will be a cold day in hell when a person with my politics is appointed to be the attorney general of the United States. The attorney general is the head of the Department of Justice, which would be better named the Department of Injustice. He (only one woman has held the job since 1789) is the chief law-enforcement officer of the United States and enforces, or does not enforce, federal criminal and civil laws, including civil rights laws. Agencies such as the Federal Bureau of Investigation (the US political police) and the Drug Enforcement Administration come under its umbrella.

Even from within a capitalist government and a legal system that currently oppresses a large majority of the population, however, the attorney general could turn this society on its head and take important steps toward an equal, freer, and less oppressive society. Ultimately, though, only under socialism will society's laws work *for* people and not as a means for protecting the ruling class.

If I did get to take the office, I would begin by not enforcing certain laws, which I'd have the right to do. Then I would investigate and prosecute the real bad guys. Here are the top ten things I'd do.

1. No prosecution of undocumented immigrants. No more criminal enforcement of immigration laws, including Operation Streamline, which has resulted in prosecution and jail sentences for scores of thousands of immigrants.
2. Handcuff the FBI, not activists. Protect our right to dissent and protest by ending FBI surveillance, spying, wiretapping, use of informants, and entrapment against activists and others not engaging in criminal activity.
3. No criminal prosecutions for selling or using drugs. Recommend the immediate parole of all persons jailed for crimes relating to drugs.
4. Recommend parole for tens of thousands in federal prisons, including those convicted as juveniles, political prisoners such as Native American activist Leonard Peltier, and Lynne Stewart and those who have served over twenty years. Those remaining should be treated humanely (no solitary confinement) and enrolled in educational programs. Ultimately, prisons must be abolished. As Ho Chi Minh said, "When the prison doors are opened, the real dragon will fly out."
5. End the prosecution of truth-tellers and Internet activists. End the persecution of people like Bradley Manning, Julian Assange of Wikileaks, and Edward Snowden; activist computer hackers like Jeremy Hammond, Barrett Brown, and the late Aaron Swartz; and untold others who seek to expose the criminality of corporations and governments and challenge corporate control of information that should be accessible to all.
6. Don't enforce the tax laws against those forced to carry the burden for the rich. The attorney general cannot change the

tax code, but he can refuse to enforce its unequal burden. No criminal prosecution or civil enforcement actions against people or families who earn under $40,000 and who refuse to pay taxes. Tax the rich, not those with lower incomes.

7. Indict and prosecute President Barack Obama and officials in his administration for murder by targeted assassination. Of the 2011 drone killing of Anwar al-Awlaki in Yemen, a federal judge recently said that the president could be subject to prosecution under a US statute prohibiting "foreign murder of US nationals."

8. Indict and prosecute George W. Bush and his torture team: former vice president Dick Cheney, former CIA head George Tenet, scores of others, and the lawyers such as Alberto Gonzales and John Yoo who tried to justify the practice.

9. Too big to fail? Too big not to be in jail. Bank and financial institutional fraud was one of the main causes of the 2008 economic crash and the recession that's continued since then. Yet 2011 saw prosecutions of financial institutions fall by half from the decade before. Prosecuting bank and financial fraud is a necessity. Another crash is inevitable under our current capitalist system, but its severity can perhaps be limited by going after the big, bad banks.

10. Propose a law similar to Bolivia's Law of the Rights of Mother Earth (La Ley de Derechos de la Madre Tierra). This law gives a legal personality to the human community and life/ecosystems. Even prior to trying to pass such a law, I would ensure that all the federal agencies under the Department of Justice protect Mother Earth and her life systems. I would enforce those rights in court by protecting indigenous communities and their cultures, along with everyone's right to water, clean air, and to live free from contamination.

In our country, capitalist law, despite its seeming neutrality, favors the wealthy over the great majority. These proposals are some of the many ways to use the law—including refusing to enforce it—to protect the majority as we make the transition to a more egalitarian society.

I can barely wait to get started in my new job.

Chapter 24

We Be Reading Marx Where We From: Socialism and the Black Freedom Struggle

Kazembe Balagun

Part I: Homegrown

In 1958, activist/singer/socialist Paul Robeson gave a sold-out performance at Carnegie Hall. The concert marked a rebirth for Robeson, who had for nearly a decade been harassed by the House Un-American Activities Committee and had had his passport taken away.

After a rousing ovation, Robeson returned to the stage and sang an encore: "Joe Hill." The song, written by Alfred Hayes and Earl Robinson, commemorates the martyred labor organizer and songsmith. When Robeson sang "I dreamed I saw Joe Hill last night / Alive as you and me / I said, "Joe, you're ten years dead" / "I never died said he," / "I never died said he," Robeson could have been discussing his own recent troubles and political resurrection.

When I listen to this concert, I realize that we in the twenty-first century are drawing from a deep well of Black radical tradition in defining our democratic institutions and who we are as a people. As artists and activists, we stand on the shoulders of giants, having the ability to mix and remix the mélange of voices that have come before us.

Socialist ideas are often portrayed as foreign to the United States and to the Black experience in particular, much as the far right lambastes President Barack Obama as a "foreign-born" "socialist." But socialist ideas are not foreign to the Black experience. They are homegrown and result from the experiences that we face as a people in this country and around the world.

The selling and trading of enslaved Africans accompanied the birth of capitalism as a global system. Slaves built the wall on Wall Street that kept the Native Americans out. The infamous "triangular trade" linked three continents: Slaves kidnapped in West Africa were taken to toil on sugar plantations in the West Indies. The sugar they harvested was shipped to New England or Britain for sale. And New England rum or British manufactured goods were traded for slaves in West Africa. Cotton grown and picked by slaves was loomed in Lancashire, England, and turned into fancy dresses for shops in Paris. The long working hours of the European working class were augmented by coffee, tea, and sugar provided by the labor of slaves on land stolen from Native Americans.

"Labor cannot emancipate itself in white skin where it is branded in black skin," Karl Marx wrote. "The workingmen of Europe feel sure that, as the American War of Independence initiated a new era of ascendancy for the middle class, so the American Antislavery War will do for the working classes. They consider it an earnest of the epoch to come that it fell to the lot of Abraham Lincoln, the single-minded son of the working class, to lead his country through the matchless struggle for the rescue of an enchained race and the reconstruction of a social world."

John Brown expressed socialist sentiments before his raid on Harpers Ferry in 1859. "All captured or confiscated property and all property the product of the labor of those belonging to this organization and of their families, shall be held as the property of the whole, equally, without distinction, and may be used for the common benefit," he wrote. He imagined a United States where all "shall be held as under obligation to labor in some way for the general good."

During the waning days of the Civil War, General William Tecumseh Sherman issued the famed Field Order No. 15, which gave formerly enslaved African Americans land in the Sea Islands of Georgia and South Carolina. This move, along with the radical program of Reconstruction to rebuild the South's political institutions after the end of slavery, laid the foundation not just for the political enfranchisement of Black people but for developing the power of white workers.

"Here for the first time there was established between the white and Black of this country a contact on terms of essential social equality and mutual respect," civil rights activist W. E. B. Du Bois wrote in his masterful *Black Reconstruction in America*. "The freeing of the nation from the strangling hands of oligarchy in the South freed not only Black men but white men."

In the 1920s, the Harlem Renaissance was closely allied with the left, specifically the Communist Party. Writer Claude McKay spoke before the Communist International, while poet Langston Hughes traveled to Russia to work on an ill-fated film on the Black experience in America. (The Harlem Renaissance also created a gay-friendly cultural space; both Hughes and McKay were bisexual.)

In the 1960s, both Malcolm X and the Rev. Martin Luther King Jr. showed signs of moving toward socialism before they were assassinated. "It's impossible for a chicken to produce a duck egg," Malcolm said at a Harlem rally in 1964, shortly after his break with the Nation of Islam and his trip to the newly independent nations of Africa. "The system of this country cannot produce freedom for an Afro-American. It is impossible for this system, this economic system, this political system, this social system, this system, period. It is impossible for it, as it now stands, to produce freedom right now for the Black man in this country—it is impossible. And if ever a chicken did produce a duck egg, I'm certain you would say it was certainly a revolutionary chicken." Asked what kind of political and economic system he wanted, he said, "You can't have capitalism without racism," and when he met white people who he felt didn't have a racist outlook, he noted, "usually they're socialists."

Dr. King, in a 1968 speech celebrating the centennial of Du Bois' birth, denounced the "irrational obsessive anti-Communism" of US politics and linked Du Bois' radicalism with his passion for justice. "We cannot talk of Dr. Du Bois without recognizing that he was a radical all of his life. Some people would like to ignore the fact that he was a Communist in his later years. It is worth noting that Abraham Lincoln warmly welcomed the support of Karl Marx during the Civil War and corresponded with him freely," King said. "Dr. Du Bois' greatest virtue was his committed empathy with all the oppressed and his divine dissatisfaction with all forms of injustice."

Later in the twentieth century, writers like Angela Davis and Audre Lorde sought to infuse socialist movements with a sensibility that would take into account the often overlooked labor of women of color. The Black-feminist Combahee River Collective, led by Barbara Smith, sought to connect those movements with those against racism, sexism, and homophobia. "We realize that the liberation of all oppressed peoples necessitates the destruction of the political-economic systems of capitalism and imperialism as well as patriarchy," it said in its landmark "Collective Statement" in 1977. "We are socialists because we believe that work must be organized for the collective benefit of those who do the work and create the products, and not for the profit of the bosses. Material resources must be equally distributed among those who create these resources. We are not convinced, however, that a socialist revolution that is not also a feminist and anti-racist revolution will guarantee our liberation."

Despite the destruction of much of the Black left by government repression, particularly the FBI's Counterintelligence Program (COINTELPRO) and the murders of Black Panther Fred Hampton (by Chicago police in 1969) and Sandi Smith (one of five communists massacred by the Ku Klux Klan in Greensboro, North Carolina, in 1979, possibly with police collaboration), socialist ideas still have resonance in the Black community. Indeed, a December 2011 Pew Research survey found that 55 percent of African Americans had a positive view of socialism, as compared to 24 percent of whites.

The reasons for this are clear. Black folks have borne the brunt of the economic recession, both in unemployment and cuts to social services. They have also borne the brunt of violence and harassment from the police, such as the stop-and-frisk policies that target Black and Brown young people and the killing of Ramarley Graham after one such incident in New York City in February 2012.

Many hip-hop artists, such as dead prez and Boots Riley of the Coup, are self-proclaimed socialists. In 1993, the Digable Planets penned "Where I'm from, nappy hair is life / We be reading Marx where I'm from." Other artists, such as Lupe Fiasco, Talib Kweli, and Erykah Badu, have championed causes of self-determination while digging at the capitalist system as a whole.

Part 2: Occupation Moment

The Occupy movement lit a fire in the hearts and minds of millions across the country. While it echoed the Arab Spring revolts in North Africa and the Middle East in 2011, it was also based deeply in the African American civil rights movement's history—in Rosa Parks' refusal to leave a bus in Montgomery, Alabama, in 1955, and the 1960 sit-ins at lunch counters in North Carolina.

Both the Occupy and civil rights movements offered glimpses of a future socialist society by creating "prefigurative" spaces and policies that reflected the vision of the world they wanted to live in. The Caribbean Marxist C. L. R. James called it "the future in the present."

The civil rights movement created alternative institutions to meet the needs of movement activists and the communities being organized. It established "freedom schools," first to challenge the bogus "literacy tests" used to deny Black people the right to vote and later to teach "people's history."

The Medical Committee for Human Rights, started in 1964 to offer first aid to injured civil rights workers in Mississippi, went on to develop clinics in the state's Black communities. Those clinics were the model for the Black Panther Party's free health clinics.

Particularly in Oakland, California, and New York City, the occupations lasted long enough for the movement to create such prefigurative spaces. In New York, the occupiers were first fed by the "pizza solidarity" movement: concerned citizens from around the world ordered pizzas to be delivered to Zuccotti Park, the small park in Lower Manhattan occupied by the protesters. This grew into full-fledged kitchens where free food was available. In the tradition of freedom schools, Occupy opened a "people's library," where young people congregated to check out books and hear open-air speeches organized by the Occupied University.

Even with the Occupy movement's tremendous accomplishments, however, many activists who called for class unity among the "99 percent" did not realize the complexity of racism in both the economics and psyche of the United States. Organizations like Occupied People of Color and Occupy the Hood urged the movement to address the long-lasting legacy of police violence, job discrimination, and prisons within Black and Brown communities.

Where solidarity was shown was in process and in action. Three personal experiences have stayed with me. The first was during the very first week of Occupy Wall Street, after the state-sanctioned murder of Troy Davis, who was executed in Georgia on September 21, 2011, despite overwhelming evidence that he was innocent and an international campaign to free him. Two days later, a massive interracial march led by anti–death penalty activists moved down Broadway. The protesters ignored the police and took the streets, and many decided to end the march at Zuccotti Park. The folks in the encampment (who numbered only two hundred at the time) welcomed them. That march was a turning point in the life of Occupy. The militancy of young activists (mostly Black and Brown) met the demands of folks fighting austerity. It was a beautiful sight.

The second came during a teach-in I organized at the Brecht Forum at the New York Marxist School, one of several there during the early days of Occupy. It was on "Organizing for Occupation: Reclaiming Housing in New York City." Afterward, a woman from Harlem explained that she had come to find support because her landlord wanted to kick the tenants out of her building and had refused to fix its boiler. Even when the tenants raised enough money to hire a repairperson, she said, the landlord refused to let them into the boiler room.

The woman presented the issue to the Occupy Wall Street General Assembly, who agreed to go to Harlem and stand in solidarity. The Occupy crew occupied her apartment building until the landlord agreed to make the repairs.

The third was in March 2012, when thousands gathered at Union Square after the murder of seventeen-year-old Trayvon Martin by a vigilante in Florida. The "Million Hoodie March" symbolized the resistance of Black youth. Martin's parents came from Florida to speak. This march also went down Broadway to Zuccotti Park. Although the occupation had ended, the spirit of freedom and solidarity remained.

Part 3: Putting People First

A day after Wall Street was occupied, my son, Miles Huxley, came into the world. I often joked that like the Occupy movement, my son was born looking messy, disorganized, and screaming for attention. And like my son, Occupy is a mixture of generations past, trying to learn how to be in the present, and looking toward the future.

In thinking about socialism through the lens of the Black radical tradition, we understand that it is connected to political, economic, and cultural self-determination. It is not something to be handed over in the distant future, but something to be created now.

The seeds of socialism can be found in organizations like the Black Food Sovereignty Network in Detroit. Detroit is a "food desert," with almost no supermarkets selling fresh food. The network has linked with farmers to bring food into the hood. It has also taken over abandoned lots for the community to grow food—by themselves, for themselves.

In Jackson, Mississippi, the Malcolm X Grassroots Movement has launched the Jackson Plan, an all-encompassing program for human rights and self-determination in the South. It aims to create a "solidarity economy," including "freedom gardens" and networks of Black farmers. The Plan also intends to create people's assemblies as democratic spaces for community control. Chokwe Lumumba, running on the Plan's principles, won election to the Jackson City Council in 2009 and is running for mayor in 2013.

Today, prison cellblocks have replaced the auction blocks of slavery in breaking up Black families, as almost a million Black people languish in American gulags. A socialist vision of the United States must articulate a new safety that includes community control of the police and the end of prisons.

Schools will be re-created. Young people will not merely sit and learn from a teacher but will be actively involved in debates on the future of society. Students will be trained and work alongside community members to figure out solutions to everyday problems. Imagine schoolchildren working alongside adults in libraries and gardens as part of their education. Everyone will learn a people's history of the contributions of Black and Brown people in the struggle for human rights.

Indeed, socialism is the unfinished chapter of the Black freedom struggle. It has been the dream of many before us. As Toni Cade Bambara once wrote, "The dream is real, my friends. The failure to realize it is the only unreality." Amen. Let's get to work.

Chapter 25

The Working-Class Majority
Speech at Occupy Wall Street, Zuccotti Park,
New York City, November 14, 2011

Michael Zweig

I bring you greetings from an earlier generation of activists. We have done this before, and we will do it again. So thank you, and we are together again here.

What the Occupy movement has done has captured the country's imagination. The reason, I believe, is that we are pointing the arrow of struggle up at the 1 percent that runs the country, not any longer down at the 99 percent who do the work. We talk about the 99 percent and the 1 percent. These are metaphors. It's important to get down to the particulars of who we're really talking about.

So who is this 1 percent? If we think about it only in terms of income, that means households who make over half a million dollars a year. In New York City, a family with a doctor and a newspaper editor might make more than half a million dollars a year. That family is not our enemy. We have to be careful in the way we formulate who are our friends and who are our enemies.

If you think about Mayor Michael Bloomberg, there is a man who is really rich. And if you think about Dick Cheney, he's also rich. When he [got] his energy committee [the US National Energy Policy Development Group] together in 2001, we still don't know who was in the room. We know they were all rich. But they were not in the room because they were rich. They were in the room because they were chairmen and CEOs and executives of big oil companies. So we have to be careful to say that this 1 percent is really the captains of industry. The high-finance CEOs and executives in finance and in industry and in commerce. That 1 percent is really less than 1 percent. It's less than half a million people in the country. But they are very powerful.

When we talk about going up against them, we have a major battle on our hands. These people do not fool around. These people can kill you. They've done it before. They'll do it again. And we have to be ready for that. And we have to think carefully, who will put a limit on the power of capital? That's where the 99 percent comes into the picture.

So who is this 99 percent? Two-thirds of them, 63 percent, are working-class people. We are dealing with a class society. That class division is not income. That class division is power. That tiny elite at the top, the tiny capitalist class, they have tremendous power. But we in the 99 percent, and especially that 63 percent who are working people, have more power. If we are organized, if we are clear about who are our friends and who are our enemies and where is the target of struggle, we can win this battle.

There is a lot of labor support for the Occupy movement. The United Federation of Teachers, a sister union of my own in the American Federation of Teachers, has been here, and we have material stored two blocks down the way, at the UFT offices. I was here the morning that they wanted to clear the park, 5:30 in the morning. There were laborers here. There were Teamsters here. There were autoworkers here. There were longshoremen here. We were here. And we kept this park! And we are still here because we have that unity. Because we have that strength among working people.

Now there is a middle class in the United States. But we are not a middle-class country. We are a working-class country. There is a middle class of managers and supervisors, of small-business owners, and of professionals, about 35 percent of the labor force. This middle class has a very divided experience. Those that are associated with the capitalist class, white-shoe law firms, Park Avenue doctors, and others in the top levels of management, have done very well in the last twenty or thirty years. But those small-business owners, those teachers, those professional people, those foremen and managers who are closely associated with working people—that part of the middle class has gone down. It has gone down with the working-class people that they serve. So when we mobilize and organize among working people, we reach out and we touch and we bring together with us those small-business owners, those managers, those supervisors, and those professional people who stand with us. Because their experience echoes some of ours.

So when we talk about challenging the power of capital, there is really only one force that can do that effectively. That's the organized strength of working people in unions and out of unions. Immigrants, native-born, white, black, Hispanic, Asian, Native American, everybody who works for a living. They are in this park, and we go to them, and we organize them with those people in the professional and managerial elements who can be on our side against this common predator, this common killer, the ruling class of this country.

Now I'm not making this up. This reflects the experience that we have in this country. This reflects the experience that people around the world have in dealing with this country. So when we address that power, it takes more than words. It takes action. Direct action. It takes disruption, disruption of the machinery of capital. Whether that's a strike or a picket line, or a mass mobilization inside some building that gets taken over, this machine must be disrupted. And if we have the organized capacity, we can prevail.

Now one central element of our campaign must be nonviolence. Absolute commitment to nonviolence. One thing that the provocateurs and the police agents and the crazy people will do is promote violence among our ranks. We have to be clear that anybody who does that, anybody who promotes that, anybody who urges that, anybody who proposes that, is not part of our ranks. That has to be. Otherwise we are opened up to the full power of the repressive state.

I want to finish up with this thought: We are out for a ferocious battle. The Reverend Martin Luther King pointed out long ago that the arc of history is long, but it bends towards justice. What we have to do is go out and bend that arc. It does not bend by itself. That is our responsibility. Now to do that we need knowledge, we need analysis, and we need people to do the work of thinking and acting together, not some people thinking and other people acting. The same people thinking and acting, deepening our understanding through our actions. That is what we need to do.

Chapter 26

How to Achieve Economic Democracy in the United States

Clifford D. Conner

"Booboisie" was the term the acid-tongued H. L. Mencken coined in 1922 to describe America's business and political leaders in an earlier era of unrestrained capitalistic gluttony. He combined "boob" with "bourgeoisie," the Marxist term for the ruling class, to depict their stupidity and greed. They were so ecstatic about raking in windfall profits from unsustainable speculation that they ignored all warnings that they were plunging headlong toward economic suicide.

The Great Depression almost destroyed the American capitalist class, but they were revived by the great economic stimulus program known as World War II. For a few decades following the war, the boobs submitted to a degree of financial regulation when wiser heads convinced them it was essential to their survival—which is to say, the survival of the free-market economic system that sustains them.

Over the last fifteen years, the booboisie have taken advantage of weakened financial regulation to rake in phenomenal fortunes from unsustainable speculation—and once again, they shattered the economy of most of the industrial world. It is tempting to encourage them to pursue their death wish and let their system self-destruct, but they could take the rest of us down too, or hold onto their power and wealth by imposing a brutal dictatorship. Most frightening are the threats of global annihilation in an ecological catastrophe or World War III. Transforming America into a country where economic justice and democracy reign is not simply a lovely dream—it is an urgent matter of survival.

Although the American booboisie hypocritically proclaim their hatred of "big government," they sit astride the largest, most powerful state apparatus in the history of the world. With their control of the armed forces, police, legislatures, courts, and election apparatus—not to mention the mass news media and the education system—their stranglehold on American society seems virtually unchallengeable. They resist even the slightest steps toward economic justice and economic democracy. So how do we get there from here?

First, there is no avoiding the word "revolution" to describe the necessary transformation. Replacing the current American economy with a system designed to fulfill the needs of human beings—all of us, and not just a few—would require a social revolution of the most profound kind.

There is also no adequate substitute for the word "socialism" to describe a post-capitalist order characterized by economic justice and economic democracy. The corporate interests that dominate the national conversation have demonized the very idea of socialism, but their monopoly will not survive the collapse of their economic system.

Revolutions are extremely risky and disruptive, which is why most sane people, aside from those who have absolutely nothing to lose, would prefer to avoid them. But the eruption of a revolution is no more a planned event than an earthquake or a tornado.

Revolutions explode when a crisis makes them unavoidable. We seem to be approaching one of those historic junctures now. When it occurs, the problem will not be how to make a revolution, but how to make sure the revolution ends in a good way.

There is no formula or recipe or roadmap for social revolutions, but it isn't completely uncharted territory. The great revolutions of the past can provide some ideas of what to expect and some clues as to what can be done to help the process along.

First, is the socialist transformation of the United States simply a utopian pipe dream? Most Americans believe that a socialist revolution could never happen here, even if they would welcome one. History, however, tells a different story. If American capitalism collapses, and it likely will, the suffering that will result could either plunge the population into the depths of despair and apathy, or it could produce a massive explosion of anger and protest. The vast majority of people might take to the streets in such conditions. It would be unrealistic *not* to anticipate that possibility.

The rise of a rebellious mass movement would not necessarily start a revolution, but it would certainly present a revolutionary situation. Whether that will lead to fundamental social change depends on whether the American people create an alternative order to replace the old regime. If the capitalist system self-destructs, that will not automatically result in socialism. The transformation to socialism cannot occur by accident or by default.

The tremendous human energy unleashed by a social crisis is like the explosively expanding steam in a steam engine. Unconstrained steam will simply expand and dissipate into the air, but if channeled to spin a turbine, it can generate the electricity to power a city.

Likewise, if the energy of a massive, angry social movement remains unfocused, it will dissipate into mindless rioting—or worse. One of the saddest lessons from twentieth-century history is that if revolutionary alternatives are nonexistent or weak, mass fascist movements can arise to fill the void. Those who recognize the need for fundamental social change should prepare *before* the anticipated social explosion to organize the mass movement.

There can be no organization without leadership. Many people have had bad experiences with self-proclaimed "leaders" who have betrayed their trust, and are understandably wary of the whole idea of leadership. But the problem of dishonest or incompetent leaders is not solved by eliminating leadership altogether. It is solved by adequate leaders coming to the fore. The successful revolutions of the past are those in which the rebellious masses could differentiate between effective leaders and false prophets.

Forms of organization and leadership do not suddenly appear out of nowhere; they emerge in the course of struggle. A revolutionary situation is a creative environment for social innovation; who can say what previously unknown forms of organization might appear? In the past, the organizations that shaped mass movements arising from social crises included trade unions, political parties, neighborhood committees, and workplace committees. To be successful, those organizations have to shield themselves from the influence of the enemies of social change by excluding agents of the capitalist class from membership. Labor unions, labor parties, and committees of the unemployed, for example, fulfill that criterion.

Such organizations will certainly not arise with the abstract ideal of socialism as their goal. They will begin with far more limited aims. In response to the massive wave of home foreclosures, for example, large numbers of determined homeowners confronting eviction-notice servers and defending each other's homes could spark a widespread movement. Militant workers could occupy factories whose owners are threatening to move their operations overseas. If their leaders are arrested for interfering with "the legal process," committees to defend them can provide another rallying point.

The need to defend and extend Medicare and Social Security, to protect ourselves from Fukushima-style nuclear disasters, to defend our teachers and our education system against the hedge fund managers' demands for cutbacks—all of these and many more could seed the growth of mass movements that challenge the guardians of the status quo.

But in the heat of a revolutionary situation, the *ultimate* goal of such movements will be to wrest control of the state away from the booboisie. The conquest of state power is the essential act of making a socialist revolution. The possibility of reconstructing society on a new, human-oriented foundation cannot begin until the stranglehold of the old ruling class has been eliminated.

Unfortunately, the booboisie will not likely be reasoned into surrendering its power and its privileges. Never in history has a ruling elite ever given up without a fight. Because they control the lawmaking bodies and the courts, they begin with the great advantage of defining the status quo as legal and those who challenge it as outlaws. They also control the means of violence—the police and the armed forces—and will certainly use them against those who defy their authority. This means that the mass movement has to be prepared to defend itself by any means necessary.

Demonstrations and picket lines can gain some security against police violence and fascist gangs by mobilizing large numbers of people. That will make would-be attackers think twice, but it is not enough. It is also necessary to organize defense guards who can protect marchers and picketers. The authorities will no doubt declare those defense guards illegal, but if they vastly outnumber the police and fascist gangs, we can ignore those legal strictures.

The most powerful and decisive weapon that a revolutionary mass movement has at its disposal is the general strike—the ability to paralyze the entire society by refusing to work. Bringing the wheels of industry to a halt (while making sure the basic needs of the population continue to be met) is the only thing that can ultimately bring the captains of industry to their knees.

A revolutionary movement's power lies in its massiveness—its overwhelming numerical superiority. Without that, the general strike cannot be general and the revolution cannot succeed. That means that "getting from here to there" is above all a *political* struggle. Before there can be a revolution, the people who will make it will have to be won over to a revolutionary political perspective. The economic crisis and injustices of capitalism will provoke a great deal of discontent, but turning that discontent into action will require a great deal of consciousness raising.

In America, a necessary step toward liberation is destroying the political monopoly of the two parties that serve the interests of the corporate elite. As long as most people can be conned into believing that the Democratic Party represents a genuinely progressive alternative to the openly pro-corporate Republican Party—or worse, into believing that the Republicans are somehow anti-elite and pro-worker—the corporate elite will remain in full control of American politics.

The two-party system will continue to delude the American public, however, until an energized mass movement shoves both the Democrats and Republicans aside. A labor party based on newly invigorated unions with new leaders infused with a fighting spirit might be one alternative. Such a party would probably not win many elections in the current billionaire-dominated system. Its most important job would be mobilizing people for far more meaningful political action than marking a ballot every year or so.

Then again, human creativity soars during periods of social ferment, so the organizational forms that arise during a revolutionary upsurge may well take everyone by surprise. What matters most is that they provide people who are ready to fight with a vehicle for making their decisions and carrying them out.

Whatever form it takes, the political alternative will have to be based on principles of human solidarity. It will have to work to overcome the myriad prejudices that keep us divided—racism, sexism, homophobia, militarism, machismo, xenophobia, anti-immigrant sentiment, and the flag-waving "patriotism of scoundrels" that applauds imperialistic conquest.

Finally, when we consider getting from here to there, what do we hope to find when we arrive? Whatever a post-capitalist, socialist future looks like or feels like, there will be some kind of structure underlying it; there will be some form of social organization to hold it all together. In a world of seven billion people, everyone simply doing their own thing is not an option. There will have to be ways to keep ourselves from bumping into one another, and there will have to be an industrial and agricultural infrastructure that can produce the things necessary to keep the lifeblood of a complex society circulating.

In the distant future, the beautiful dream in which the state has "withered away" may become a reality. But the socialist era cannot begin without a state. The booboisie, in its desire for absolute freedom to accumulate profit, has poisoned the public's perception of "big government," but no modern society can exist without big government. The real issue is not whether a big government is necessary, but whose interests it will serve—a tiny layer of billionaires, or the vast majority of the population?

That majority would have much better lives if it could dismantle the economic system based on institutionalized greed and replace it with a planned, cooperative economy. That is the essence of socialism. But who will do the planning? A revolutionary leadership in the twenty-first century will have two powerful negative examples: the Soviet Union and China, bureaucratically planned economies ruled by repressive one-party regimes. To avoid that, governmental forms will have to institutionalize control from below rather than rule from above. When the present world order disintegrates, struggling to create socialist democracy will be the only alternative to descending into the abyss of fascism.

So there you have it. We have to prepare for the possibility that a forthcoming capitalist meltdown will create a revolutionary situation and set a mass movement into motion. As it is developing, that mass movement will have to be steered toward a socialist solution. Then it will have to be organized enough to defend itself, implement a general strike, and take state power, and then to reorganize society along democratic socialist lines.

This is a very neat scheme, a very simple concept, but it will be extremely difficult to translate into reality. At every step along the way, a thousand surprises await us. But what choice will we have?

Chapter 27

The Capitalist Road: From Chinese Sweatshops to Detroit's Decay

Dianne Feeley

In the United States, capitalism promotes the myth of the lone individual who rises to the top, overcoming all obstacles through innovation and hard work. The most recent incarnation was Steve Jobs, celebrated as the Thomas Edison of his era, whose technological creativity transformed how we communicate. By his death in 2011, Jobs had amassed a personal fortune estimated at $7 billion.

Jobs was a packaging genius who tightly controlled every aspect of the production and distribution process. His corporate model relied on highly paid managers and designers and, beneath them, a loyal army of low-paid retail employees. It contracted production out to companies in China where workers labored seventy to eighty hours a week in order to meet demand. Sometimes coerced into round-the-clock shifts, these workers had to stand for so long that their legs swelled.

For Apple, this system worked well. In the last quarter of 2011, it made $13.06 billion profit on $46.3 billion sales. Had overseas suppliers been able to produce more, Apple executives noted, it would have had still greater profits.

Since the news surfaced that several factory workers had committed suicide, Apple has been shamed into signing on to a code of conduct for suppliers. But the stressful conditions didn't occur overnight. While Apple lavished attention on every product detail—with Jobs famously insisting that the iPhone's front panel be made from glass instead of plastic so it would not get scratched—the fate of its workforce was not a consideration. We now know that in 2009–10, 137 workers were poisoned by breathing in hexane, a component in gasoline that was used to clean the glass on iPhones. It's much more toxic than alcohol, but it dries faster.

Corporations don't focus on the well-being of their workforce unless workers collectively make demands or publicity reveals their working conditions. Capitalism, after all, is a social and economic structure where everything is for sale and best obtained at bargain-basement prices. Consequently, it builds an unequal, violent, and increasingly unsustainable society.

The people who organized Occupy Wall Street rejected this hierarchy. In their declaration, they expressed their solidarity in the face of "mass injustice" and aligned with those who are "wronged by the corporate forces of the world." They saw the problem as a systemic one.

Built Into the System

Although many assume that this economic system and the social relations that flow from it suit people's competitive nature, capitalism has only been around for a few hundred years. It is a dynamic system centered on market production and continual expansion. Capitalists own the means of producing goods or services (the physical space and appropriate technology) and have access to capital and raw materials. Banks are an essential part of the system because corporations need financial resources. For an enterprise to expand, it needs a flow of capital to buy raw materials, hire more workers, introduce new production methods, purchase more sophisticated machinery, gobble up other companies, or move into other markets.

Credit enables corporations to survive bad times. Capitalists also often use economic crises as an opportunity to drive down wages or purchase at depressed prices companies or resources that might later come in handy. While some capitalists lose out, others are strengthened.

Workers, however, do not possess industrial machinery, raw materials, or capital. We must therefore sell our ability to work: our "labor power." The majority of us perform production, transportation, or services for the 1 percent who own the means of production and distribution. Under capitalism, labor power is a commodity that, like any other commodity, is exchanged on the market. When that doesn't happen, one remains unemployed, unable to obtain what is necessary for survival.

What is unique about labor power is that within the unit of measure—calculated in time—the worker can be motivated or coerced to work faster or produce a higher quality commodity. It is human labor that transforms raw materials into commodities to be sold on the market. For this reason, capitalists and their managers zero in on how to streamline, speed up, or reorganize the process so workers will produce more efficiently.

Karl Marx, who spent his life dissecting the dynamics of capitalism, described the workday as divided into two distinct parts. In the first, the worker produces a value equivalent to his or her wage. In the second, production continues, but all value goes to the employer. Marx termed this portion unpaid labor, or the "surplus value" that the employer keeps. Out of this, the capitalist pays for the upkeep of the facility, the materials used, and interest on the money borrowed. What is left over is the profit.

Capitalists and workers need each other, but the power relationship is skewed. They also have different goals. The workers' goal is to sell labor power in order to have money for commodities we need to live. (Marx summarized this process as "C-M-C": the worker sells his or her labor power—a special kind of a commodity, but a commodity nonetheless—to earn money. With that money, workers purchase the commodities that enable them to survive.) For the capitalist, the object is to purchase labor power in order to be able to sell a commodity and increase one's capital. (Marx's formula for this was "M-C-M": the capitalist begins with money, invests it to produce a product or service—a commodity—and then sells what is produced for more than their original investment.) Without the capacity to make profit, the capitalist would cease production.

Capitalists, of course, may have a problem realizing their profit, because they usually can't sell commodities or services until after they've been produced. If the product sits on the shelf, its value cannot be realized. It may be useful (and therefore has "use value"), but because it has not been exchanged, it has no "exchange value." Of course, the capitalist may be able to recoup some value by reducing the price, but this cuts into potential profit.

Capitalism is a dynamic and ruthless system in which the search for new markets, lower costs, and higher quality drives innovation. When I worked at Ford in the 1970s, more than a million autoworkers produced thirteen million vehicles for the US market. Today, while production is approximately the same, two-thirds of those jobs are gone. In the seventies, every worker on the shop floor earned more or less the same hourly wage. In today's Ford plants, there are long-time workers who still have decent pay and benefits alongside newer workers who earn half their pay with fewer benefits. But there are also temporary workers, who can be dismissed at any time, and contract workers, who may have been working at the plant for years but are not officially Ford employees and therefore don't acquire seniority. All of them work at a more intense pace than I did in the 1970s.

The method of production has also changed, with more automation and fewer skilled workers who repair machinery or maintain the facility. More parts are produced by outside suppliers. While Ford has had plants all over the world since the 1920s, those plants used to produce for the local market. Today they are part of the global production process.

Once the Big Three—General Motors, Ford, and Chrysler—dominated the US auto market, but their decision to stick to producing mainly large cars even after the gas-price increases of the 1970s and their failure to adopt new production techniques caught up with them. They began losing market share, particularly to smaller, higher-quality Japanese cars. During the recession of the early 1980s, the Big Three and the United Auto Workers complained to Washington about this. The Reagan administration got Japan to limit the number of vehicles it exported annually to the United States. Except for a short period, this did not decrease the competition with US auto companies. Instead, it facilitated the establishment of "transplants": foreign-owned auto factories in the United States.

Over the past thirty years, these transplants have installed their production and distribution methods; won generous tax credits to build factories, primarily in low-wage Southern states; and staved off unionization by paying wages comparable to unionized facilities—but without the benefits. Their management-by-stress model taught the Big Three that the Ford model of a smoothly running assembly line was overstaffed. "Just in time" delivery was another innovation, reducing the costs of warehousing and, even more important, reducing excessive inventory and the capital tied up in it.

Toyota became the model—so much so that when Washington bailed out General Motors and Chrysler in 2009, the Obama administration stipulated that their labor costs should not be more than the average in the transplants. While Ford and GM represented the model of production during the first three-quarters of the twentieth century, the revolution in communication and transportation systems has established a new global model.

Today, the entire global supply chain, from manufacturer to retailer, uses standardized bar codes, scanning devices, computerized inventory management, and automated distribution centers. Big-box retailers like Walmart, which offer easy one-stop shopping, have detailed knowledge of what they have in stock and which items are selling. Selling products for less than their smaller competitors, they are now in the driver's seat. The size of their orders lets them dictate every aspect of the product, from its labor cost to its quality and delivery date. Corporations like Walmart, Apple, and Nike are so lean that they do not even own their own factories. This is the face of early twenty-first-century capitalism.

Although popular culture might focus on an individual capitalist as "greedy," the reality is that if a capitalist enterprise does not increase its profitability, it will be overtaken by other corporations. Walmart has expanded from Southern rural areas to urban centers and into countries as different as Britain, Mexico, and China. Its labor costs are only 15 percent of its total sales, roughly half the usual amount for department stores. And in Walmart's drive to expand its profits, it also demands that its suppliers reduce the cost per unit or improve product quality each year.

This model of lean production and retailing has been emulated across a range of industries, from transportation and communication to health care and even the US Postal Service. Before World War I, Ford advertised jobs at $5 a day to encourage workers to stay on. Today, companies like Walmart and Amazon *depend* on part-time and temporary workers. Their annual turnover is about 40 percent. As one Amazon temp remarked, "We are disposable."

Whatever the form of capitalist production, workers must sell their labor power. Thus we are forced to submit to the owner's dictates about the work process, hours of employment, job assignment, and company rules. Because we have no control over our work, workers are constantly alienated by our on-the-job experiences. "He does not count the labor itself as a part of his life; it is rather a sacrifice of his life," Marx wrote in *Wage-Labor and Capital*. "It is a commodity that he has auctioned off to another."

Workers confront alienation and exploitation in differing ways. Some wall off their work life from what they see as their "real" life. Others find great satisfaction in "stealing" time or materials from the boss. A few numb themselves with drugs or alcohol. The corporate media teach us to judge other workers as "lazy" and therefore undeserving. Once this mainly applied to looking down on lower-paid workers or the unemployed—particularly when they had darker skin—but today it applies to better-paid workers, who are seen as living off the fat of the land at the expense of the lower-paid worker. These feelings keep us divided and alone in our alienation. But even when we cannot articulate how we feel, workers desire an end to the exploitation and alienation we experience.

US Capitalism's Evolution

Capitalists need a state that will defend their private property interests, mediate conflict through legislation or repression, levy taxes in order to finance its programs, and negotiate relations with other countries to gain advantages for the enterprises of the home team. But not all capitalists have the same perspective. No single corporation or cartel owns the government outright. Its policies are shaped by competition among different factions of capitalists. They are also shaped by being forced to intervene in conflicts between workers and capitalists.

Governments can ease class conflict by regulating working conditions, by raising the minimum wage, and through policies and programs that transfer money to working, unemployed, and retired people. They can also take sides against workers by reducing benefits such as unemployment compensation, passing laws that inhibit unionization, or failing to raise the minimum wage. Today's federal minimum, $7.25 an hour, buys much less than the $2.90 minimum did in 1979.

When I was a child in the 1940s and 1950s, more than one-third of US workers belonged to unions. Union organizing and strikes won wages and benefits that got their members a portion of an industry's productivity gains. However, they failed to overturn the Taft-Hartley Act of 1947, which narrowed union rights and did not successfully campaign to unionize the still segregated South.

Starting in the early 1950s, corporations moved their operations out of the industrialized cities. Instead of union jobs raising the wages, benefits, and working conditions of nonunion workers, the opposite occurred. By 2010, only 6.9 percent of the private-sector workforce was protected by union contracts, compared with 36.2 percent in the public sector. (That is the biggest reason for the vicious attacks on public workers today.)

Since the recession at the end of the 1970s, US capital has been able to change economic and political life to the disadvantage of working people. At first, the unions agreed to concessions under the assumption that they were temporary. But corporations continued to demand more givebacks under the pretext that the battle for market share required them. As early as 1978, UAW President Douglas Fraser labeled this as "a one-sided class war." Yet more than thirty years later, the union leadership still supports another round of retreats. They say—and many workers agree—"at least we still have jobs."

In the twenty-first century, capitalism has become increasingly mobile. Instead of making long-term investments in plants and machinery, it overbuilds facilities and then pits one workforce against each other. It can also outsource production to subcontractors to take advantage of lower wages, weaker worker-safety and environmental rules, tax breaks, and more lucrative regional markets or market niches.

But what does it mean for a corporation to close down a facility? It is not just about the loss of jobs for individual workers and their families. It is a loss for the community as well. As a Detroiter, I can testify to what that looks like.

Detroit as a Model

Detroit has been an important national industrial area since the Civil War. Known for its ironwork, it was once the "stove capital of the world." In the twentieth century, it became the Motor City, the world leader in producing autos and trucks, and the Big Three ranked among the United States' biggest and most solidly profitable businesses. But beginning in the 1950s, its largest factories began closing down, moving to the suburbs, or leaving the area. Although there are still steel plants, auto-parts suppliers, and assembly plants within the city, their workforce is relatively small. And since these are the better-paid jobs, many of those workers live in nearby suburbs. Deteriorating factories and polluted land dominate the city. The population is disproportionately poor, black, elderly, disabled, and unemployed.

With a declining tax base, the city could not maintain its services. Various mayors responded by dolling up the downtown and letting the neighborhoods fend for themselves. In the last decade alone, a quarter of Detroit's population left the city. Since 2005, banks have foreclosed on 67,000 properties. In the Motor City, a third of the residents don't have cars, but the partially privatized bus system is near collapse. In January 2012, a report issued by a coalition of community groups found mold or filth in one-third of the city's grocery stores; 38 percent sold food past its sell-by date. The worst violators were concentrated in poorer African American neighborhoods with a higher proportion of children. As a consequence, many Detroiters trek to the suburbs to shop.

Despite these serious problems, the city continues to be a vibrant musical and artistic center. We have more than 1,600 community gardens, and fruit and vegetable markets are springing up. Newspapers suggest the unemployment rate is between 30 and 50 percent, so it's clear that Detroit needs sustainable jobs. Yet there is no plan at the local, state, or national level to turn this situation around. Instead, fueled by the media and politicians, public opinion views Detroit as a black-majority city that needs to learn how to live within its means.

To teach this lesson, the state disenfranchised Detroit by leaning on local elected officials until they agreed to let a financial board oversee the city's financial downsizing. It dictated the terms under which city employees would work and ordained the selling of city-owned assets as well as combining, shrinking, outsourcing, or privatizing government departments that run public services. Only police and firefighting are deemed core services.

By March 2013 Governor Rick Snyder appointed bankruptcy lawyer Kevyn Orr as the city's emergency manager. Orr announced that his job was to take the city through an "Olympics of restructuring." He explained that all the city's resources could go up for sale in order to cover the city's $15-18 billion debt— including the animals in the zoo, the artwork at the Detroit Institute of Arts (DIA), Belle Isle and the city-owned but regionally operated Water Department.

In an interview with the *Wall Street Journal*, Kevyn Orr summarized the history of Detroit's problems: "Detroit has been the center of more change in the twentieth century than I dare say virtually any other city, but that wealth allowed us to have a covenant [that if] you had an eighth-grade education, you'll get thirty years of a good job and a pension and great health care, but you don't have to worry about what's going to come."

He was quoted as saying "for a long time the city was dumb, lazy, happy, and rich." Surprised that people would find these comments offensive, Orr tried to backpedal. But Orr believes what he said—that the working people who came to Detroit to find jobs and a better life were dumb to believe that they had the right to a good job. We were dumb to believe that after we won the battle to turn Detroit from an open-shop city with low wages into a union town, capital would allow that situation to continue. We were dumb to believe capital would remain—don't we know that capital is always reinventing itself, moving on to new markets, new opportunities?

Much has been written about the possible sale of the DIA's artwork, but the restructuring plan as it is emerging is focused on attacking the benefits of the city's 30,000 current and retired workers. More than 8,000 police officers and firefighters draw pensions averaging $30,000 a year (they do not draw Social Security); almost 12,000 city workers receive an average pension of less than $20,000. They also receive city-paid health care, although they now have co-pays and deductibles. Currently there are also 10,000 city employees entitled to benefits. They have already taken a 20 percent pay cut and must pay 30 percent of their health insurance coverage.

Although the Michigan constitution protects pension benefits, Orr, by filing for bankruptcy, plans to treat retirees as "unsecured creditors," whose pensions might be worth ten cents on the dollar. Retiree health coverage would be cut altogether.

The city's two separate pension funds oversee $7 billion in investments. If they are found to be less than 80 percent fully funded, Orr can dismiss the pension board and allow the state treasurer to appoint a sole trustee. The actuarial levels are in dispute, with Orr's consultants claiming they are vastly underfunded. However Detroit's pension system is in better shape than those of many other cities, and superior to the state system. Clearly having control over these funds opens up investment opportunities for capital.

While Orr stopped paying city contributions to the pension fund, he committed the city to spending a minimum of $22 million to hire restructuring consultants. Between the time Orr was hired and he started working, Jones Day—his former law partners—were awarded a $3.35 million contract to develop a restructuring plan.

What won't be investigated by the Orr team is the role the banks played in destabilizing the city through manipulating credit ratings, encouraging city officials to borrow at variable rather than fixed rates, and foreclosing on homes, devastating large swaths of the 140-square-mile city.

Many talk of Detroit's coming gentrification, but that will be limited to the downtown area. Even as Orr sues to take the city into bankruptcy, more than $300 million in state funding will be made available to build a hockey stadium near the baseball and football arenas.

Detroit, however, is a city of neighborhoods. These have been starved of resources, including the shuttering of more than one hundred public schools. Except for a brief period, the Detroit public schools have been taken over by the state, in one form or another, since 1999.

The results include a ballooning school debt, more school closings, more teacher layoffs, increased class sizes, constant turmoil, and the growth of charter schools with nonunion staff. Only about one-third of Detroit's 150,000 school-age children are still enrolled in the city's public schools.

The latest innovation will remove fifteen of the "worst-performing schools" and place them under an Education Achievement Authority. When negotiations over the 2012 teachers' contract deadlocked, the schools' emergency manager, former GM executive Roy Roberts, simply imposed one. Detroit public schools are now on their third emergency manager. We are now saddled with a huge debt the state has run up. In fact, to start up the EAA, the authority secretly borrowed several million dollars from the Detroit public schools and lied on their application for grants. Had the Detroit school board functioned this way, criminal charges would have been brought against them.

Detroiters believe that the determining factor in the state's intervention was that it is a majority-black city. The smaller Michigan cities and towns where emergency managers have been imposed—Flint, Pontiac, Benton Harbor, Hamtramck, and Ecorse—have also been deserted by corporations; their remaining residents are also poor or people of color. (Michigan voters repealed the emergency-manager law with a union-backed ballot initiative in November 2012, but the state legislature passed a new one during a lame-duck session in December, and Governor Rick Snyder named a new "emergency financial manager" for Detroit in March 2013.) But while the jobs were disappearing and the need for social services increased, state and federal governments significantly reduced aid to local governments.

Working Hand in Hand

Capitalism works for the 1 percent, but it's a disaster for the rest of us. We are told there is no money for jobs, wage increases, public services, or social programs, yet there *is* money for the corporations and the things they see as essential:

- State and federal governments have cut corporate taxes as well as taxes on the 1 percent. According to the Congressional Research Service, the Bush tax cuts of 2001 and 2003 alone cost an estimated $3.5 trillion.
- The wars in Iraq, Afghanistan, and Pakistan have cost between $3.7 and $4.4 trillion. Justified as wars on "terrorism," they are instead a major investment by US corporate interests in gaining control over areas that produce oil and natural gas.
- Since 9/11, US spending on "homeland security" has more than tripled. According to John Mueller and Mark Stewart's 2011 book, *Terror, Security and Money: Balancing the Risks, Benefits and Costs of Homeland Security*, it has consumed $1.1 trillion in direct and indirect costs.
- By 2010, the cost of the bank bailouts had reached $12.8 trillion in loans and guarantees, one Bloomberg News reporter estimated.

These costs surpass the $20 trillion the US government will owe by 2019. Why should we accept this debt as legitimate? Why should this debt put our future in a straitjacket?

Instead, we need to reverse the inequality that hampers our society. We also need work—meaningful work—that benefits our society. It's clear that these options will not come out of Washington or our state capitals, so we need to take matters into our own hands.

In 2011, Detroit Mayor Dave Bing set up a number of meetings across the city to talk about our city's future. A few thousand people attended, eager to get involved—only to discover canned presentations with a hidden agenda. People were angry and disgusted.

However, the experience reinforced my view that people *want* to participate in planning. We don't need another blue-ribbon panel, but rather a people's audit. We could organize people's assemblies to look at our city budgets or investigate the national one, with working committees to research various aspects of the finances, particularly the debt owed to large banks and investors. Did borrowing this money enable the government to expand a needed service, or did it go to waste or corruption? Did bank officials demand to be first in line for repayment? What portion of the debt is the interest on previous debts? Were there extra charges because the city or state's credit rating was downgraded? And did government officials make deals that caused additional bank charges? In Detroit, the city's investments in hedging derivatives will end up costing more than a billion dollars.

These committees would also look at the sources of revenue. Detroit's revenue has been declining for sixty years, yet state politicians pronounce the need for austerity as if the problem was a recent spending spree. In reality, many interrelated factors have caused this problem: corporations abandoning factories, thereby lowering the amount of taxes collected and leaving behind toxic waste dumps; cuts in corporate tax rates; corruption; a high rate of evictions and foreclosures that in turn reduced the amount of personal property taxes collected; less revenue returned by the state; and less federal money allocated to cities and corruption.

Once we in the community empower ourselves through understanding how the system currently works, we will demand change. Some residents would undoubtedly want to meet with officials and present demands to renegotiate various debts. Others will organize and join marches, teach-ins, and occupations at banks and corporations. Getting evictions suspended would be a first step toward restabilizing the community.

Instead of fixating on electing an individual to be their representative, we would come together to deliberate as our own governmental body—because *we* are the ones who need to be in charge. These local committees and assemblies would organically help develop regional and national networks, meetings, and coordinated actions.

Unlike current government processes, a people's audit would be transparent. In examining expenses and assets, people will need to evaluate the social obligations we have as a community. For example, if education is a fundamental obligation, how do we create quality schools? In such an open and democratic process, hiring the least expensive and most overworked teachers won't be the goal. Ridding schools of art, music, learning a variety of skills, or physical education in favor of more testing would be viewed as just plain nuts.

How can we create useful jobs? Does a corporation have the right to shut its doors, lay off the workforce, remove equipment, and flee the community? Some cities have attempted to stop corporate closures by arguing in court that the company received tax breaks but failed to fulfill its promises. These cases have been unsuccessful, so more activist avenues will have to be pursued.

One interesting model to consider is the handful of successful plant occupations that have taken place in Ontario, Canada, over the last few years. While they were limited to securing plant-closing agreements, they asserted that workers have a stake in the facility. But if you consider the stake that the surrounding community has and not just the immediate workforce, giving corporate property rights privileges over the substantial claims of this community makes this a limited victory.

Armed with this concept of plant occupations, workers and the community in cities and towns throughout the Midwest could take over plants slated for closing or even those that had already been shut. In some cases, they might continue production—but it would also be a unique opportunity to manufacture alternative-energy products. The axle factory where I worked until my retirement had almost 2,000 employees. Today it stands empty, one more idle plant in a city of empty plants. Yet an axle plant could be easily retooled to produce wind turbines.

We cannot afford one more plant closing or one more foreclosure. We can no longer afford an economic system that pollutes our land, air, and water; endangers our food supply; and reduces biodiversity. At every turn, this system is at odds with our survival.

The Occupy movement shed light on a new perspective. While the big occupations of 2011 are gone, we have vibrant eviction defense committees in a number of cities. In Detroit, we have held mass vigils to prevent the sheriff from carrying out evictions, while we try to shame and pressure the banks and the Federal National Mortgage Administration (Fannie Mae) into working out mortgage modifications. We have gone door to door in neighborhoods and held open meetings on the front lawns of people threatened with eviction. These direct actions are necessary to force the banks to reconsider their demand to foreclose, to publicize our actions, and to build a compelling alternative.

We have grown up in a capitalist society, so we find it hard to imagine a different reality. The truth is that this one is at a dead end. A people's audit, beginning at a local level, can start us on the road to considering other possibilities. It isn't a revolution, but without developing the basic tools to solve problems together, we will remain paralyzed, waiting for someone to come along and save us.

Our organizations and practices must be transparent and democratic: it is only through transparent and democratic practice that we will learn to analyze, innovate, evaluate, and work together. These skills, combined with direct action, will give us the confidence to displace the powerful, profit-driven system that threatens our future.

Chapter 28

The Third American Revolution: How Socialism Can Come to the United States

Paul Le Blanc

Socialism could be defined as economic democracy. It means rule by the people over the economic structures and resources that we need to keep ourselves alive and healthy, to engage in creative activity, to maintain good relationships with one another, and to have good and meaningful lives. This is a revolutionary goal. It means a fundamental change from an economic dictatorship—an economy owned and controlled by a small capitalist minority for the purpose of maximizing its profits—to an economy owned by all, democratically controlled by all, and planned and coordinated to meet the needs of and provide for the free development of all.

What Socialism Is Not, and What That Means for How to Get It

To reach this goal, we have to clear away a serious misconception about what socialism is. Socialism is not a benevolent state that decides how best to take care of us, like some imperious parent.

If that were socialism, then it could be achieved by a relatively small number of very smart people taking control of the state and using it to take care of us. Perhaps this benevolent minority would come to power through a violent upheaval, establishing a "people's republic" ruled by a revolutionary party that would oversee the far-reaching and positive changes. Or perhaps the benevolent minority would be elected and gradually develop an elaborate conglomeration of governmental institutions that would oversee resources and policies to shape our lives in better and better ways.

But who would decide what is "positive" and what is "better"—and how would they decide? How would these benevolent "educators themselves be educated" (a question Karl Marx posed so pointedly in 1845), and why would we trust them with our lives and future? If they had so much power, what would keep them benevolent? Some of the worst crimes in history have been committed by people who exercised power over others in the name of socialism. (Similar crimes have been committed in the name of freedom, democracy, and innumerable religious creeds.)

Democracy and freedom are at the heart of socialism. It involves people taking control of their own lives, shaping their own futures, and together controlling the resources that make such freedom possible. This change will need to emerge naturally from the way that we struggle to bring the hoped-for society into being. Socialism will come to nothing if it is not a movement of the great majority in the interests of the great majority. Humanity needs no condescending saviors. People can only become truly free through their own efforts.

Three American Revolutions

Another challenge for getting from the capitalist "here" to the socialist "there" is finding things in our present-day capitalist society that can make the transition possible.

We have had two previous revolutions in American history: the American Revolution of 1775–1783, and what some historians have called the Second American Revolution, the Civil War of 1861–1865 and the Reconstruction that followed it. The first ended the British king's rule over the thirteen colonies and forged them into the independent United States of America, a republic within which many people would continue to struggle to realize the revolutionary democratic ideals enshrined in the Declaration of Independence. The second ended slavery in this would-be democratic republic, reemphasizing (for example, in the Gettysburg Address) the revolutionary ideals proclaimed at its founding.

In those revolutions, masses of people engaged in momentous struggle brought about a fundamental power shift. They ended the rule of certain powerful and privileged classes, of the British upper crust and monarchy, and the wealthy plantation-owning slavocracy. Many US socialists have argued that we must undertake a third American revolution that would end the economic dictatorship of capitalism and establish rule by the people over our economy.

These earlier revolutions are part of what has formed our society today, and their experiences provide resources for shaping the next phase of our history. But they emerged from the complex social, economic, and political realities of their times. We have to understand those realities in our time if we want to effect a third American revolution.

Possibilities of Socialism Here and Now

There is fantastic potential for socialist transformation today. Our economic resources and technologies are currently being used to maximize the profits for the 1 or 2 percent of the people who own the economy in order to give them greater and greater wealth and economic power. If these resources were used less wastefully, less irrationally, and more democratically, they could provide the material basis for a better society in which everyone could live a life of dignity, community, creativity, and freedom.

The economy's functioning depends on a socially organized labor force that draws together the elemental life force, the strengths, the abilities, the knowledge, the skills, and the expertise of many millions of people. This diverse mass of individuals keeps our economy running. Without them, nothing would be possible.

To understand what this means and why it is important, let's set aside the fuzzy-minded concept of the "middle class"—those who are not rich and not poor, but somewhere in the middle. The slogans of the recent Occupy Wall Street movement captured the stark realities of economic power much better: the wealthy and powerful 1 percent ruling at the expense of the other 99 percent of the population. The math may be slightly off—one could argue that the top levels should be seen as 3 percent, with another 5 percent or so as their very loyal and highly paid managers, advisors, and assistants. The rest of us—be our pay high or low, whether blue-collar, white-collar, or "professional" employees, whether in the private or public sector—are the force whose labor makes it possible for our society to exist and survive. This massive labor force could be even bigger and more productive, as millions of people are unemployed, underemployed, or poorly employed because those who control the economy have concluded that it would be unprofitable or less profitable for things to be otherwise.

The members of this working class, which includes their family members and dependents, constitute the great majority of people in our society. Because of their numbers and their role in our economy, together they have immense potential power. They also have an obvious capacity, given their social organization, to provide the basis for a socially owned and democratically controlled economic system.

Despite these possibilities, there is no pathway to socialism if a majority of the people do not want it. The capitalist minority uses its immense economic might to secure power over our government (including both major political parties, the military and police, and the ways our laws are shaped and understood); over our news media, educational systems, and culture; and, in innumerable other ways, over the day-to-day lives of the great majority of people.

This adds up to an immense amount of power. Since the coming of the Industrial Revolution to the United States—since the 1820s—there have been many eloquent socialists and militant labor insurgencies in this country, and sometimes they have had significant impact. But they have never been strong enough, no matter how much they appealed to the great working-class majority, to replace the economic dictatorship of capitalism with the economic democracy of socialism.

The Power and Weakness of Capitalist Ideology

Whether the working-class majority consists of 99 percent or 92 percent or 63 percent of the people, a key to the power of those who want to maintain the capitalist status quo can be found in the working class itself. It involves the violation of the old adage "United we stand, divided we fall." The working-class majority consists of hundreds of millions of individuals, of men and women, young and old and in-between, native-born and immigrant, LGBT and straight, of many different ethnic groups and races and mixtures. As the great American poet Walt Whitman once said, we are "a nation of nations." They have many religious differences—and some have no religion. They vary as to regional cultures and cultural tastes. Such differences have generated friction, intolerance, and fear among different groups, and led to hateful dehumanization.

The minority of people who own and control our economic system have some such differences among themselves, but they often find ways to tolerate them, especially if such unity allows them to work together to protect their economic and political power. This powerful elite has also proved quite adept at nurturing deep and multiple antagonisms around such differences among various sectors of the working class: "Divide and conquer!"

Some members of the working-class majority even embrace, celebrate, and aspire to the power and greed of the wealthy capitalist minority. They may admire the more powerful and identify with them vicariously, or even justify the very behavior that oppresses them. They may believe that if they are smart enough and work very hard that someday they, too, can rise to the ranks of the wealthy—that the rich are rich because they are smart and hardworking and that those who are not rich are generally stupid and lazy and deserve their economic hardships.

Yet over time, such notions ring hollow for many. They see stupidity and sloth among the rich and the powerful. Most of the rich inherited their wealth, and those who are not rich can rarely realize any hopes of becoming wealthy. Most people who work hard and are smart end their lives with accumulated weariness and, perhaps, wisdom, but not wealth. The hard knocks of reality persuade significant numbers that while some may be fortunate to find a job that provides a decent living, not all people can rise into the top 1 or 2 or 3 percent, no matter how hard they work. Ronald Reagan (after working his way up to his own perch of wealth and power) once commented, accurately, on the plight of the lower classes: "Whoever said that life is fair?" The many smart and hardworking people for whom Reagan's pathway is closed understand increasingly clearly that this is a fundamental truth of capitalist society.

More than this, people in this diverse, working-class majority usually hold elemental beliefs that are intrinsically socialist. Most believe deeply that our society should be animated by "liberty and justice for all" and should have a "government of the people, by the people, and for the people." Most believe, as is written in the Declaration of Independence, that governments are legitimate only if they enjoy the consent of the governed and that all people are entitled to "life, liberty, and the pursuit of happiness." Most believe that there should be "equal opportunity for all." Most identify with the Golden Rule: "Do unto others as you would have them do unto you." Most are disgusted by the truth inherent in the joke about the Golden Rule: "He who has the gold makes the rules."

Politicians of both major political parties, from all across the political spectrum, have found it necessary to give considerable lip service to these radical democratic ideals and values in order to be elected. Policies that contradict such values must be clothed in the rhetoric of those ideals in order to gain any popular acceptance.

The problem for capitalist ideology is, as Abraham Lincoln is alleged to have said, "You can fool all of the people some of the time, and some of the people all of the time, but you can't fool all of the people all of the time." Another way of putting it is: reality trumps hype. The actual dynamics of real-world capitalism erode the belief in this economic system that enriches the few through the exploitation of the laboring majority. This system may have created many wondrous advantages for society, but its negative qualities pollute our culture and our environment, and it periodically intensifies "austerity" and hard times for the majority of the people, even as the rich get richer.

How Gains Are Made and Consciousness Changed

Many of those in our diverse working class who have come to the conclusion that capitalism is not fair and fouls things up are discouraged by the powerful notion that there is nothing we can do about it. The history of our country shows that this is not true. But much of our history is unavailable to most people. What passes for history is all too often collections of trivia having little to do with the actual lives of real people, or tedious recitations of partial truths and pseudo-facts designed to buttress the status quo. Those whose wealth gives them predominant influence in our cultural and educational systems prefer to keep it that way.

The history of the United States has been shaped and punctuated by struggles for freedom and social justice. As Frederick Douglass, the great anti-slavery orator and organizer, so perceptively said in 1857:

> The whole history of the progress of human liberty shows that all concessions yet made to her august claims have been born of earnest struggle. . . . If there is no struggle, there is no progress. Those who profess to favor freedom, and yet deprecate agitation, are men who want crops without plowing up the ground. They want rain without thunder and lightning. They want the ocean without the awful roar of its many waters. This struggle may be a moral one; or it may be a physical one; or it may be both moral and physical; but it must be a struggle. Power concedes nothing without a demand. It never did and it never will. Find out just what a people will submit to, and you have found out the exact amount of injustice and wrong which will be imposed upon them; and these will continue till they are resisted with either words or blows, or with both. The limits of tyrants are prescribed by the endurance of those whom they oppress.

This was true of the struggle against slavery, the struggle for independence, and the struggles to make the new republic more democratic. It was true of the working class's struggles for better wages, better working conditions, a shorter workday, and what we now call the weekend. It was true of the struggle for women's suffrage and their struggle to overcome the many forms of degradation to which they have been subjected. It was true of the struggle to resist and overcome Jim Crow segregation laws that subjugated African Americans for more than a century after slavery was abolished.

None of these gains fell from the skies or were granted through the benevolence of the upper classes. None of them simply crystallized through the workings of the market. They came about through struggles waged by highly organized social movements that were able—with great persistence against immense obstacles—to work profound changes in popular consciousness, mobilize popular pressures, and bring together great social forces that forced those who had power to give way.

The great movements that shaped the history of the United States during the twentieth century—the labor movement, the civil rights movement, and the movement to end the US war in Vietnam—were comprised of men and women influenced by and committed to socialist ideals, both in their central leadership and among their most dedicated activists. This was no less true of the resurgent struggles for women's rights and among the pioneers of the movement for gay and lesbian rights. These socialists' organizational knowhow, sense of history, analytical skills, and broad social vision helped to build effective social movements that won important victories and stimulated thinking and shifts in consciousness among the growing numbers of people involved in the mass struggles that brought about social change.

"I know there was a Socialist Party and a Communist Party helping to organize," autoworker Nellie Bessons-Hendrix said after the successful union struggles of the 1930s. "Although I never belonged to a party, I feel that had it not been for the education and knowhow that they gave us, we wouldn't have been able to do it." She was involved in the Women's Emergency Brigade during the great Flint, Michigan, sit-down strike of 1936–37, in which hundreds of autoworkers occupied General Motors factories for weeks and forced the company to recognize their union, the United Auto Workers.

"Our policy was to organize and build strong unions so workers could have something to say and assist in changing the present order into a socialist society," explained V. R. Dunne, a leader in the successful Minneapolis general strike of 1934, during which a handful of experienced militants, inspired by the revolutionary socialist ideas of Leon Trotsky, became active in the Teamsters Union.

In this way, the powerful notion that there *is* something we can do about it develops among those in our diverse working class who have come to the conclusion that capitalism is not fair and fouls things up. And "reform" and "revolution" are not incompatible goals, despite all the ink, keystrokes, and hot air expended pitting them against each other. The actual revolutionary socialist movement—not only in the United States during the 1930s but in the whole world over more than one hundred years—has seen them as part of the same process. As Rosa Luxemburg, a German socialist leader in the early twentieth century, put it, the movement understands "the struggle for social reforms as its means, and the social revolution as its aim."

A Movement of the Great Majority, for the Great Majority

These movements' experience points to one basic principle: socialism and the working class cannot move forward unless they are interconnected through the struggle for democratic rights and social justice for the multifaceted working-class majority. Inseparable from this is the understanding that freedom cannot be fully won except through one's own efforts. Only the working class can bring about the liberation of the working class, and this can only be achieved fully by replacing the economic dictatorship of capitalism with economic democracy.

This is different from liberalism, which usually favors political democracy and social reforms but embraces the economic framework of capitalism. Socialists have made common cause with liberals in numerous social struggles, but liberation cannot be won simply by supporting reform-minded candidates of a pro-capitalist party. Experience has shown over and over again that being tied to such candidates will inevitably cause movements to veer away from socialist insights and the strength of independent mass action. The obvious pressure on socialist supporters of a liberal candidate is to avoid doing anything that would undermine that candidate's "electability" and his or her ability to secure financial support from big-money donors.

The revolutionary socialist relies on the developing consciousness and power of a mass working-class base to win reforms and pave the way for mass socialist consciousness and a socialist future. The key is to build social movements and struggles that are independent of any pro-capitalist politicians. While some members of such movements will support such politicians, the movement as a whole will need to remain independent in order to remain effective, to put pressure on all politicians while being in the hip pocket of none.

It may be that sincere liberals rely on "lesser-evil" politicians rather than on the pressure of mass action because they don't have confidence in the activist potential of the working class. This also seems true of some revolutionary-minded anti-capitalist activists disinclined to support politicians at all. Instead of building mass struggles of working people (often dismissed as the "numbers game"), they engage in their own militant actions—for example, property damage and street fighting—that preclude broader participation and can confuse or alienate broad sectors of the working-class majority.

These actions by relatively small groups are different from the militant actions and nonviolent civil disobedience of the labor and civil rights movements, which involved large numbers of people or were organically connected to the broad struggles of a large strata of the population. Substituting one's own militant actions for such mass action both makes activists vulnerable to victimization by the authorities and undermines the possibility of effectively reaching the people whose numbers can actually help to win the struggle.

In the United States today, there is a broad array of forces that could crystallize into a mass socialist movement: working-class people who want to fight back against capitalist austerity measures (lower wages, cuts to public education and mass transit, threats to Social Security, etc.), radicalized trade unionists, environmentalists and Green Party supporters, veterans of the Occupy struggles, assorted left-wing groups, activists against various forms of racism and bigotry who see links between human rights and economic justice, people who are tired of seeing money that should go to human needs being spent on militarism and military adventures, and the growing number of others who are frustrated and furious over economic injustices that are coming down on them.

This could be the basis for a broad left-wing coalition that agrees on certain basic principles (and agrees to disagree on certain differences). Such developments seem to be crystallizing in various countries. As British activist Owen Jones suggests, it might be possible to "link together workers facing falling wages while their tax credits are cut; unemployed people demonized by a cynical media and political establishment; crusaders against the mass tax avoidance of the wealthy; sick and disabled people having basic support stripped away; campaigners against crippling cuts to our public services; young people facing a future of debt, joblessness, and falling living standards; and trade unions standing their ground in the onslaught against workers' rights."

Activists seeking to prepare the way for a socialist future face the challenge of developing tactics, educational and organizing efforts, and overall strategies to build a mass movement that can win meaningful victories now while preparing the way for the working-class majority to come to power and bring a fundamental change from capitalism to socialism. They will have to discuss, debate, and define what electoral activities, street actions, and other means will help achieve that end.

There will be useful lessons to learn from other movements and struggles, both historic and recent, both in the United States and other countries. There will undoubtedly be unique new possibilities and resources that activists can draw upon in deciding what is to be done. But if there is to be a genuine possibility of a genuinely socialist future, the guiding thread must be how best to build a movement of the great majority that can bring about the triumph of the great majority.

Chapter 29

Imagine the Angels of Bread

Martín Espada

This is the year that squatters evict landlords,
gazing like admirals from the rail
of the roof-deck
or levitating hands in praise
of steam in the shower;
this is the year
that shawled refugees deport judges
who stare at the floor
and their swollen feet
as files are stamped
with their destination;
this is the year that police revolvers,
stove-hot, blister the fingers
of raging cops,
and nightsticks splinter
in their palms;
this is the year
that dark-skinned men
lynched a century ago

return to sip coffee quietly
with the apologizing descendants
of their executioners.

This is the year that those
who swim the border's undertow
and shiver in boxcars
are greeted with trumpets and drums
at the first railroad crossing
on the other side;
this is the year that the hands
pulling tomatoes from the vine
uproot the deed to the earth that sprouts the vine,
the hands canning tomatoes
are named in the will
that owns the bedlam of the cannery;
this is the year that the eyes
stinging from the poison that purifies toilets
awaken at last to the sight of a rooster-loud hillside,
pilgrimage of immigrant birth;
this is the year that cockroaches
become extinct, that no doctor
finds a roach embedded
in the ear of an infant;
this is the year that the food stamps
of adolescent mothers
are auctioned like gold doubloons,
and no coin is given to buy machetes
for the next bouquet of severed heads
in coffee plantation country.

If the abolition of slave-manacles
began as a vision of hands without manacles,

then this is the year;
if the shutdown of extermination camps
began as imagination of a land
without barbed wire or the crematorium,
then this is the year;
if every rebellion begins with the idea
that conquerors on horseback
are not many-legged gods, that they too drown
if plunged in the river
then this is the year.

So may every humiliated mouth,
teeth like desecrated headstones,
fill with the angels of bread.

Chapter 30

Thanksgiving 2077: A Short Story

Terry Bisson

I was first, as the eldest and the closest, in a way. I had lived with Grandpa and "Uncle" Johnny through my teens after both my parents were killed in the fighting in Philly. My cousins hadn't enjoyed that distinction.

The old house looked run down, but hey, so did Grandpa. He was sitting on the porch, rolling a cigarette, and I noticed that his hands were a little shaky.

"You're smoking?" I didn't even try not to sound disapproving.

"Only temporarily, Emma," he said. "Meanwhile, give me a hug."

That wasn't hard. He was skinny as a rail and his cigarette smelled a little funny. I suspected he had called us together for more than one reason and, alas, as it turned out, I was right.

He even let me help with the cooking. All that morning I was in and out of the kitchen as my cousins arrived. By 11:55 Grandpa had us all around the big oak table.

"The turkey is almost done," he said. He insisted that we put aside our phones and pads to catch the official ceremonies on TV. An old union man (IWW 2.0), Grandpa was nothing if not patriotic.

Somebody-or-other Rodriguez, the Congress rep from Mississippi (the watershed, not the state) was giving thanks for the progress in wetland restoration, income adjustment, voter communication, littoral evacuation . . .

"Progress *in* means problems *with*," grumbled Les, our litigator. "Sometimes I think that all socialism changes is the words."

Grandpa laughed. "That's something to be thankful for," he said. "I can remember when income adjustment wasn't even in the country's vocabulary."

"Neither was littoral evacuation," complained Jesse, our youngest.

We all joined hands around the table for the national anthem, "This Land is Your Land." Even Howard, our tuneless scholar, sang, but only after observing that he'd like it better if an Indian had written it instead of a settler.

The prayer, at least, was short and sweet. "So ecumenical it's almost free-range," quipped Wendell, our agricultural atheist. Then Grandpa turned off the TV and disappeared into the kitchen. He returned with the turkey. "Free-range too, of course!"

"Of course," muttered Les. "How else can you keep them so skinny?"

"No complaints, please!" said Grandpa, beginning to carve. "This is Thanksgiving, and at least everybody gets one these days."

"Without standing in line at a soup kitchen," I added. Then I brought in the biscuits. That got a few cheers.

We all chowed down. Grandpa opened the wine, which thankfully was a nice California red. In DC all we get these days is Virginia, thanks to all the overzealous local locavores.

"I'll go first," said Grandpa, raising his glass. "By giving thanks for all my lovely contentious grandchildren who have graciously interrupted their lives to join me here today. Who's next?"

"I'm thankful that I got here at all," groaned Lydia, our linguist, who can groan in six languages. "I'm working as a translator at Immigration Pediatrics in Atlanta, enrolling refugees, and I had to explain to two separate committees why I needed three days to attend a two-hour dinner, and then it was an all-nighter on a slow bus detouring around the smoke plume from the Colorado wildfires."

"No complaints, please. We're all thankful that you made it as well," said Grandpa. "Next?"

"I'm sixty percent thankful that the fires are sixty percent under control at last," said Mark, our brigadier, who was working off his student debt in a fire crew. "I was out there trenching and hauling water until just last week. Luckily, I had a furlough coming, and Annie gave me a ride."

"You have a car?!" We all stared at Annie, not so much jealous as amazed.

"Of course not," Annie said, our do-gooder. "But our senior-care collective does. We need it for the home visits. I told a white lie and got it for the weekend, but I have to be back early Monday."

"What's a white lie?" asked Jesse.

"A harmless lie," said Grandpa. "And I'm sure Annie's thankful that the homeless all have homes. Who's next?"

"I'm thankful that the drought is easing," said Wendell, our country cousin. "The North Prairie corn crop looks good, and I'm thankful that we saved enough heritage seed to get us through. And I'm hopeful for the future. Our GMO teams are developing corn that grows on vines! No more ripping the topsoil every year. Though I'm going to miss the old John Deere."

"Now that you're done plowing under the family farm," grumbled Les. "Willie Nelson must be rolling over in his grave."

"Willie should roll less and read more history," said Howard. "The family farm was just a mechanism for child labor. They needed the nine-month school year so the kids could be put in harness. Plus the big cooperative farms are the best way to avoid chemicals and grow organics. How you going to feed the world otherwise?"

"If co-op farms are so good, how come we only eat meat twice a week?" grumbled Les.

"So others around the world can eat it once a week," said Grandpa. "What kind of world would it be if half the people were skinny so the other half could get fat?"

"Plus, raising meat is wasteful," said Wendell. "Think of a pig as a calorie sink."

"Yesterday's waste is today's wealth," said Katie, our optimist, who operated a backhoe for Resource Management. "Landfill mining can be tedious, but I'm thankful that we have all this plastic to reprocess now that petroleum is under UN interdiction."

"Thank you for that thanks," said Grandpa. "How about you, Rebecca? What are you giving thanks for today?"

"Family," she said, our housewife. "I love you all, but Frank should be here too. He's been up in Alaska since June with the UN team tearing out those stupid pipelines. They were supposed to be done last month."

"The wildlife protocols at work!" said Grandpa. "You should be proud."

"I guess I am," she said. "And with three kids, I'm getting paid for childcare, so that helps. Though sometimes I wonder, who cares about a bunch of stupid caribou anyway?"

"The other caribou?" offered Grandpa. "Your turn, Jane. Any visits from the muse?"

"She wouldn't know where to find me. I'm with a Commons Restoration team, painting bridges and taking out fences, which means a lot of travel. The good news is, I finally got that novel-writing grant I applied for two years ago, so I get one week off a month next year."

"We should all give thanks for that," said Grandpa. "Socialism needs great literature!"

"Actually, it's science fiction, not literature," said Jane.

"Even more essential," said Grandpa. "How about you, Nathaniel? What are you thankful for this Thanksgiving?"

"The Grim Reaper," said Nathaniel, our computer nerd. "Don't look at me like that, I'm serious. I'm thankful that the pre-Rev dinosaurs are dying off, mostly of old age, even though scheduling their rants on People's Access still takes up half my workweek. Ten to twelve hours a week at least."

"Even dinos have a right to be heard," said Grandpa, who was proud to be a liberal, especially now that it was a bad word again.

"Not only a right but a responsibility," said Nathaniel. "When this new electoral protocol is approved, everyone will be required to log in and vote at least once a week, not only locally but nationally."

"In the old days," said Howard, "most folks didn't even bother voting. The candidates were chosen for them by advertising."

"What's advertising?" asked Jesse.

"Harmful lies," said Grandpa. "What about you, Cecelia? Have you finished your Brigade service?"

"Last August," said Cecelia, who had been working off a degree in environmental architecture from Stanford@Tulsa. "But now I'm thinking of going back to college."

"Anything beats working, I guess," mumbled Les.

"Study is work," snapped Cecelia. "I'm going back because I got inspired by my Brigade work in day care. I thought it would just be tying shoes for toddlers. But the architecture of human intelligence is fascinating. If I get accepted, I'll be working with the top minds, the best scientists in the country."

"Not to mention the best bucks," grumbled Les.

Cecelia smiled and shrugged. Child development is in the highest quadrant of the USSA's four pay grades.

"Wish I was in some kind of development," said Jesse. He had always wanted to be a cop or a lawyer, but since there was little call for either these days, he had joined the Brigade right after high school. "I thought infrastructure would be building stuff," he said. "Not just tearing down prisons and dams. And now I'm stuck in Florida. The evacuation and resettlement is almost done, but we still have to haul off all their crap before it washes away and pollutes the fisheries."

"Can't blame the rising seas on socialism," said Grandpa. "If we'd dismantled capitalism earlier, we could have stopped global warming. Or at least slowed it. Now half your work is damage control."

"There is a good side even to that," said Howard, currently a Zinn scholar with Harvard@Nashville. "I'm writing a paper arguing that the transition to socialism was easier since the government was more involved with disaster relief than war. More peaceful, for sure."

"Somewhat," grumbled Les, who had lost an eye in the Baltimore Courtroom Assault. "But I doubt many folks would have gone for socialism if they had known it meant downsizing."

"How many would have gone for capitalism," said Grandpa, "if they had known that it required continual mindless expansion?"

"Billions," mumbled Les. "People are stupid and greedy."

"Capitalism might have worked," said Alita, our starstruck dreamer, "if only the planet had gotten bigger every year."

"It seemed, for a few centuries at least, that it did," said Howard. "The discovery of the "new world" meant that Europeans could . . ."

"Zzzz," said Jesse, dramatically slumping his head onto the table, next to the gravy bowl.

"All right, no more history lessons," said Grandpa. "Your turn, Alita. That sweet smile tells me you have something to be thankful for."

"I do," said Alita, who was just finishing her doctorate in astronomy from Columbia@Tucson. "I got my Brigade assignment last week, and it runs concurrent with my post-doc."

"Which means?" we all asked.

"Two years as a lunatic."

"Gingrich?" Grandpa sounded more jealous than amazed. He was always a science-fiction fan.

"Bingo! Next month I leave from Baikonur Equatorial for the dark side of the moon. I'll be on the rocky worlds team. Interning at first, then who knows?"

"Congratulations," said Howard. "Though I still can't believe the UN's moon base was named for that nutty old reactionary."

"Even a stopped watch is right once a day," mumbled Les.

"Twice," said Alita.

"Let's not argue, children. Now let's hear from Emma, who made this delicious apple pie."

"Apple-rhubarb," I said. "I'm thankful that Marge and I finally got the go-ahead from Local Peripherals to open our restaurant. Now I can use the cooking skills you and Johnny taught me on something more interesting than stew for restoration teams."

"Meatless mulligan," mumbled Les.

"I hear it wasn't so bad," said Grandpa, opening the last bottle of wine. "And now it's my turn."

"No complaints!" we all chimed in.

"I'm thankful that screw-tops have finally replaced corks. And that community control has finally replaced private ownership. That decisions are being made by people instead of by capital. That we have an economy based on sustainability instead of growth. That nobody can cut an ancient tree or foul an aquifer just to make a buck."

"So you're actually a conservative!" teased Howard.

"Always was," said Grandpa. As if to prove it, he began rolling a cigarette. "Socialism is about conserving the planet for future generations."

"You're smoking?!" We all complained in one voice. All but me. I'm slow but I was catching on, neither amazed nor surprised. Just dismayed.

"Allow an old man his vices. I will only be indulging them for a few more months. I won't be around for next Thanksgiving, which is why I brought you all together. A bit of a farewell."

There was a long silence. Which I broke.

"So it's back," I said.

"Cancer is like capitalism, Emma. All it knows how to do is grow. You can only live with it so long."

"What about the canadas?" Annie protested. That's what we call the neighborhood clinics. "Can't they send you up to Oncology?"

Grandpa shook his head, more than a little sadly. "To Hospice. I'm an old man, kids. Medical resources are limited like everything else, and the world is filled with young folks who need it more than a geezer who's almost eighty. It's only fair that I move aside. Pass on, as they used to say."

It was Lydia who burst into tears. "That was my white lie! I said I was going to my grandfather's funeral."

"Now you're an honest woman again," said Grandpa. "I'm thankful for that. And for the good years with Johnny. And especially for the privilege of growing old, for living long enough to see the beginnings of a new age, not just here but in the world. So no complaints, please."

"Goddamn it," said Jesse. "Some Thanksgiving."

"I'll take that complaint as a compliment. Now since I can't smoke in the house, out of respect for Johnny's rules as well as common law, perhaps some of you will join me on the porch."

We all did. I brought out coffee. Fair-trade, of course. Grandpa's funny-smelling cigarette was only half tobacco, so he passed it around. Then he passed out fidels, which we were told we could keep in his memory, or smoke if we wished.

I have plenty of memories, more than a girl deserves, so I dried my eyes on my apron and lit mine.

So did Les.

"Cuban," he remarked. "And every bit as good as ever."

Both amazed and surprised, I sat down beside him and rapped him on the head. It was so hard it hurt my knuckles. "So what do you say?"

"Thanks."

Chapter 31

You Are the Light of the World: Speech Via Mic Check at Occupy Wall Street

Joel Kovel

You are the light of the world.
I'm not saying this to flatter,
but because we have to understand it deeply.
Your genius has been to seize upon the emerging hopes
 of humanity—
and give them a form of realization.
Now you are on the threshold of a world-transforming
 process,
and you must decide whether to cross over it.
Most of you have been spurred to come here by
 economic and political injustice:
Vicious indebtedness, precarious employment,
 unemployment, a nightmarish rise in inequality of
 wealth.
In short, the workings of a system that is corrupt,
 manifestly broken, and, it seems, in terminal crisis.
But that is just one side of the problem, and, I fear, the
 lesser side.

The brutal fact of the other side is that our planetary
   ecology is breaking down.
Climate change, species loss, widening circles of
   pollution are some of its marks.
All this and more testify to
an ecological crisis of unprecedented proportion that
   threatens the future of civilization,
and even the extinction of our species along with many
   others.
It is the greatest challenge in all human history.
To meet it we need to begin with a basic truth:
That the same system that causes economic and political
   injustice
also causes ecological breakdown.
It follows that to understand and change both sides of
   our predicament,
we need to be able to name and understand this
   system—
and first of all to see it as a system
and to understand its root,
so that we can uproot it.
The system, in a word, is capitalism.
Capitalism is more than the set of corporations,
though corporations are among its instruments.
It is a deep-seated ailment in the human condition
that centers around the conversion of everything to
   money
and lives from the expansion of money, or profit, which
   becomes capital itself.
This expansion is inherently endless, because money is
   number, and number has no limit.
We call this "capital's accumulation," and it is the
   supreme value of the capitalist system.

To accumulate, capital has to start somewhere.

This takes place in something called a Commons.

A Commons is a portion of nature collectively worked on
and enjoyed by people.

When the capitalist class takes control of the Commons,
it's called an enclosure.

Thus the history of capitalism can be written as an
ongoing and expanding series of enclosures—
and the struggles against this.

When the European settlers came here they saw that the
Indians were communists who lived according to the
Commons.

This aroused their vampire-like greed and so they set out
on a path of destruction and possession.

They enclosed the Commons, put walls around it, and
converted it to private property.

And yes, Wall Street is named for a real wall built on the
actual site of today's street.

It defined an enclosure built to "wall off" the Algonquin
Indians
and keep them out of the settlers' way.

This can be said to be the launching point of capitalism
in North America.

It has grown into the metastasizing cancer known as
"finance capital" you see all around you,
extending everywhere to the outer limits of empire,
and into the depths of our souls.

Indeed, the name, "Wall Street," has come to mean
capitalism itself.

So you see, when you occupy Wall Street you are truly
reversing the enclosure of Commons and tearing at the
very root of capitalism.

Welcome to the Indian Nation!

And this, friends, is the secret to your stroke of genius
    that makes you the light of the world.
If we are faithful to this lesson, we can transform society,
    bring about justice for all,
and overcome the ecological crisis.
For you have created a pathway of "commoning."
Your space of occupation is both a site of resistance and
    a site of production.
This dual nature is what gives strength and resilience to
    your movement
and ignites the spark to inspire the whole world,
even as you have been inspired by other examples of
    creative commoning.
Now a resistant and productive commons is itself a
    flourishing, integral ecosystem,
and the building ground for healing and restoring other
    ecosystems.
It is implied in what Karl Marx wrote in 1848—
and I hope you are not ashamed to learn from Karl Marx—
that we will build "an association in which the free
    development of each is the condition for the free
    development of all."
Therefore freedom is the essential condition for a society
    beyond capitalism.
An association of free people will take care of nature
because they see themselves as part of nature.
They will struggle for a new world based on a new kind
    of production that gives nature intrinsic value.
They will develop the tools for overcoming and healing
    the cancer of accumulation
and the ecological crisis it generates.
Such a society will be in harmony with nature and not
    nature's enemy.

I would call it "ecosocialism,"
and I hope you will join in its building.
The task is fantastically difficult.
But once you realize that
you are not here to want what they want you to want:
to help out the Democratic party;
to get a seat at the big table;
to rationalize the deadly regime of accumulation . . .
new choices open before you.
And this choice, this is the one for the flourishing of life.
Neither are you here to want what I want you to want.
You are here to seize the day whose dawning you have
   brought about,
and to direct it into the future.
Much study lies ahead,
much frustration, indeed, much sacrifice . . .
but also much joy—
once you accept the truth that the old order is dying
and the faith that a new one can be born.

This poem is taken from a speech delivered October 28, 2011,
at the Occupy Wall Street encampment in Zuccotti Park.

Contributors' Biographies

Mumia Abu-Jamal, a renowned Philadelphia journalist, has been incarcerated since 1981 for allegedly shooting police officer Daniel Faulkner. For years, he has received international support in his efforts to overturn his unjust conviction. This movement forced his removal from death row after almost thirty years, but he is still facing a life sentence. He cofounded the Philadelphia branch of the Black Panther Party at age fifteen. Later, he was a radio reporter for stations WHYY and WHAT and became known as the "Voice of the Voiceless" for covering the city's poor. He is the author of *Live from Death Row*, *Death Blossoms*, *All Things Censored*, *Faith of Our Fathers*, *We Want Freedom*, and *Jailhouse Lawyers*.

Tom Angotti is a professor of urban affairs and planning at Hunter College and the City University of New York Graduate Center and directs the Center for Community Planning & Development (www.hunter.cuny.edu/ccpd). He is author of *New York for Sale*, *The New Century of the Metropolis*, *Accidental Warriors*, and other books. He coedits *Progressive Planning* magazine and remains actively engaged in struggles for environmental justice and the "right to the city." He worked in government and was a Peace Corps volunteer in Peru in the 1960s.

William Ayers is formerly Distinguished Professor of Education and Senior University Scholar at the University of Illinois–Chicago and a founder of the Small Schools Workshop and the Center for Youth and Society. His articles have appeared in numerous scholarly and popular journals. His books include *Teaching Toward Freedom*; *A Kind and Just Parent*; *Fugitive Days*; *On the Side of the Child*; *Teaching the Personal and the Political*; *To Teach: The Journey, in Comics* (with Ryan Alexander-Tanner); *Teaching Toward Democracy* (with Kevin Kumashiro, Erica Meiners, Therese Quinn, and David Stovall); and *Race Course* (with Bernardine Dohrn).

Kazembe Balagun is a writer, cultural organizer, and communist who lives in the Bronx. He currently serves as director of education and outreach at the Brecht Forum in New York City and has been featured in *The New York Times*, *Time Out New York*, *L Magazine*, and the *UK Guardian*.

Ajamu Baraka is a longtime human rights activist and veteran of the Black Liberation Movement. He has been in the forefront of efforts to develop a radical, people-centered perspective on human rights and to apply it to social justice struggles. He was the founding director of the US Human Rights Network; serves on the boards of the Center for Constitutional Rights, Africa Action, and the Mississippi Workers' Center for Human Rights; and is the board chair of the Latin American and Caribbean Community Center. He currently is working with the Black Left Unity Network, is a fellow at the Institute for Policy Studies, and is the editor of *The Fight Must be for Human Rights: Voices from the Frontline*.

Terry Bisson is a Hugo Award–winning science fiction writer who lives in California. A veteran of the John Brown Anti-Klan Committee (NY), he is the author of biographies of Nat Turner and Mumia Abu-Jamal, as well as an alternative history of the Civil War, *Fire on the Mountain*, in which Harpers Ferry is a win. His latest novel, *Any Day Now*, is set in a 1968 that might have been.

Renate Bridenthal is a retired professor of history at Brooklyn College, the City University of New York. She has coedited and contributed to various books: *Becoming Visible: Women in European History* (1977, 1987, 1998), *When Biology Became Destiny: Women in Weimar and Nazi Germany* (1984), *The* Heimat *Abroad: The Boundaries of Germanness* (2005), and the forthcoming *The Hidden History of Crime, Corruption and States*.

Since 1965, **Leslie Cagan** has worked in a wide range of peace and justice movements in New York and nationally. Her organizing skills have helped mobilize hundreds of thousands of people in public protest, including the million-person nuclear-disarmament march in New York in 1982, the historic lesbian/gay rights march on Washington in 1987, and the largest mobilizations against the war in Iraq between 2003 and 2007. Her major organizing projects have included efforts to normalize US-Cuba relations; she has also organized against police brutality and for budget equity. She led United for Peace and Justice, the nation's largest coalition against the Iraq War. Her writings have appeared in nine anthologies and in scores of journals, newspapers, and online outlets.

Mat Callahan is a musician and author from San Francisco now residing in Bern, Switzerland. He composed and performed music with seminal world-beat band the Looters, whose success led to the founding of the artists' collective Komotion International. For eleven years, Komotion was a center of radical art-making and revolutionary politics in San Francisco. Its performance space, art gallery, and sound magazine brought together artists and activists from around the world. He is now organizing a revival of James Connolly's "Songs of Freedom." He is the author of three books: *Sex, Death and the Angry Young Man*; *Testimony*; and *The Trouble with Music*. He can be contacted at info@matcallahan.com or www.matcallahan.com.

Clifford D. Conner is on the faculty of the School of Professional Studies at the City University of New York Graduate Center, where he teaches history. He is the author of *A People's History of Science* (Nation Books, 2005) and has written biographies of two eighteenth-century Irish revolutionaries, *Colonel Despard* (2000) and *Arthur O'Connor* (2009). His most recent book, also a biography, is *Jean Paul Marat* (Pluto Press, 2012). He is also on the editorial board of *The International Encyclopedia of Revolution and Protest* (Blackwell, 2009).

Blanche Wiesen Cook is University Distinguished Professor of history and women's studies at John Jay College and the Graduate Center, CUNY. Her books include *Crystal Eastman on Women and Revolution* (Oxford University Press, 1978); *The Declassified Eisenhower: A Divided Legacy of Peace and Political Warfare* (Doubleday, 1981); and *Eleanor Roosevelt*, a three-volume biography (Viking-Penguin, vol. 1, 1992; vol. 2, 1999; vol. 3, forthcoming). She has also served as the American Historical Association's vice president for research and on the boards of the Feminist Press and *Science and Society*. She cofounded the Peace History Society and the Fund for Open Information and Accountability, and is a life member of WILPF.

Angela Davis is an activist, writer, and Distinguished Professor Emerita of the history of consciousness and feminist studies at the

University of California–Santa Cruz. Her work as an educator—both at the university level and in the larger public sphere—has always emphasized the importance of building communities of struggle for economic, racial, and gender justice. She is the author of nine books; the most recent is *The Meaning of Freedom*. Having helped to popularize the notion of a "prison-industrial complex," she now urges her audiences to think seriously about the possibility of a future world without prisons and to help forge a twenty-first-century abolitionist movement.

Martín Espada is the author of more than fifteen books. His latest collection of poems, *The Trouble Ball* (Norton, 2011), received the Milt Kessler Award and an International Latino Book Award. His previous collection, *The Republic of Poetry* (Norton, 2006), was a finalist for the Pulitzer Prize. The recipient of fellowships from the Guggenheim Foundation and the National Endowment for the Arts, Espada teaches at the University of Massachusetts–Amherst.

Dianne Feeley is active in Occupy Detroit's eviction defense committee. A retired autoworker, she is a member of Autoworker Caravan, a group of rank-and-file autoworkers who oppose concessions and urge that idle factories be converted to produce mass transit and non-fossil-based energy. She is an editor of *Against the Current*, a bimonthly socialist magazine.

Harriet Fraad is a psychotherapist and hypnotherapist in private practice in New York City. She publishes in *Truthout*, *Tikkun*, *The Journal of Psychohistory*, and *Rethinking Marxism*. Her recent book, *Class Struggle on the Home Front*, was written with Stephen Resnick and Richard Wolff and edited by Graham Cassano. Harriet writes a regular blog with Richard Wolff, "Economy and Society," at RDWolff.com/econ_psyc and on her own Web site, HarrietFraad.com.

Tess Fraad-Wolff, LMSW, CAT, is a psychotherapist at the Center for Psychological Well-Being in New York City. Her latest work, "Capitalist Profit and Intimate Life," appeared in the *Journal of Psychohistory*, [winter 2013, (40): 1].

Frances Goldin heard the word "socialist" when she was eighteen and met her husband-to-be, Morris Goldin. It sounded like a great idea. She got married at twenty, when her activism began, and at age eighty-nine, it hasn't stopped yet. In 1959, she helped organize New York's Lower East Side community to beat city development czar Robert Moses and save the Cooper Square neighborhood and its thousands of residents from urban renewal. She founded The Frances Goldin Literary Agency almost forty years ago, and it's still going strong, favoring books that help change the world. Now, she says, "Let's free Mumia!"

Juan Gonzalez is a staff columnist for the New York *Daily News* and cohost of *Democracy Now!*, a daily morning news show broadcast by more than one thousand community and public radio and television stations. His investigative reports on the labor movement, the environment, race relations, and urban policy have garnered numerous accolades, including two George Polk Awards for commentary. He has written four books, including *Harvest of Empire: A History of Latinos in America,* and *News for All the People: The Epic Story of Race and the American Media.* He was a leader of the Young Lords Party in the 1960s and of the National Congress for Puerto Rican Rights in the 1970s. He has also served as president of the National Association of Hispanic Journalists.

Arun Gupta is a cofounder of *The Indypendent* and *The Occupied Wall Street Journal* and former international news editor of the *Guardian* newsweekly. He is a contributor to *The Guardian*, Salon,

The Progressive, Truthout, and Alternet, and has been profiled by *Business Week*, PBS, *Wired*, and *The New York Times*. He received a Wallace Global Fund grant for his work with the Occupy movement and is a Lannan writing fellow. He is a regular commentator on *Democracy Now!*, the Canadian Broadcasting Corporation, Al Jazeera, and Russian Television. He is writing a book on the decline of American empire for Haymarket Books. He is also a graduate of the French Culinary Institute and cooked professionally in New York City.

Fred Jerome is the author of *The Einstein File: J. Edgar Hoover's Secret War Against the World's Most Famous Scientist* (St. Martin's Press, 2002), *Einstein on Israel and Zionism* (St. Martin's Press, 2009), and, with Rodger Taylor, *Einstein on Race and Racism* (Rutgers University Press, 2005). He has also written for *Newsweek, Technology Review*, and the *New York Times*. In the early 1960s, he covered the exploding civil rights movement in the South. His reporting from Cuba for the *National Guardian* earned him two subpoenas from the House Un-American Activities Committee and was subsequently denied a passport by the US State Department. In 1979, he created the Media Resource Service, a telephone referral service that enabled journalists to ask questions of more than 30,000 scientists. More recently, he has taught at the Columbia University School of Journalism, New York University, the New School, and the Brecht Forum.

Melanie Kaye/Kantrowitz is a writer, poet, activist, scholar, and teacher. She taught the first women's studies course at the University of California–Berkeley, where she earned a PhD in comparative literature. She has taught Jewish studies, women's studies, urban studies, race theory, public policy, and queer studies all over the United States. For five years she directed the Queens College/CUNY Worker Education Extension Center in Manhattan.

Her books include *The Colors of Jews: Racial Politics and Radical Diasporism*; *The Issue Is Power: Essays on Women, Jews, Violence, and Resistance*; and *My Jewish Face and Other Stories*. She was the founding director of Jews for Racial and Economic Justice and cofounded *Beyond the Pale*, its program on Pacifica's WBAI-FM.

Joel Kovel, originally trained as a physician and psychoanalyst, has played a leading role in the emerging ecosocialist movement through *The Enemy of Nature* (2002, 2007), editing the journal *Capitalism Nature Socialism* (2003–2011) and cofounding organizations such as Ecosocialist Horizons. His other books include *History and Spirit* (1991) and *Overcoming Zionism* (2007). In the 1980s, he began working with radical priests in Nicaragua, and in 2012 he formally converted to Christianity, joining the Episcopal Church.

Paul Le Blanc, a professor of history at La Roche College in Pittsburgh, has been active in various movements for social change since 1965. He is coauthor with Michael Yates of *A Freedom Budget for All Americans: Recapturing the Promise of the Civil Rights Movement for Economic Justice Today*. His other books include *Work and Struggle: Voices from US Labor Radicalism*; *Marx, Lenin and the Revolutionary Experience: Studies of Communism and Radicalism in the Age of Globalization*; and *A Short History of the US Working Class: From Colonial Times to the Twenty-First Century*.

Dave Lindorff is a veteran award-winning investigative reporter and author. His first book, *Marketplace Medicine: The Rise of the For-Profit Hospital Chains* (Bantam, 1992) explored the perverse effect of corporatization on this key part of the nation's health-care system. A graduate of the Columbia University Graduate School of Journalism and a two-time Fulbright scholar who has lived and worked in Hong Kong, China, and Taiwan, he has seen various health-care systems at work firsthand in these and many other countries. A freelance writer for the last thirty-three years, he is also founder of the online newspaper This Can't Be Happening! at www.thiscantbehappening.net.

Michael Moore is an Academy Award–winning filmmaker and best-selling author. His films *Fahrenheit 9/11*; *Capitalism: A Love Story*; *Bowling for Columbine*; and *SiCKO* are among the all-time top ten grossing documentaries. His most recent book is *Here Comes Trouble: Stories from My Life*. His Web site is www.michaelmoore.com.

Frances Fox Piven is on the faculty of the City University of New York Graduate Center. Together with Richard Cloward, she is the author of *Regulating the Poor*, *Poor People's Movements*, *Why Americans Still Don't Vote*, *Challenging Authority*, and *Who's Afraid of Frances Fox Piven?*

Michael Ratner is president emeritus of the Center for Constitutional Rights (CCR) in New York and is chair of the European Center for Constitutional and Human Rights in Berlin. He and CCR are the attorneys in the United States for Julian Assange and Wikileaks. He is still trying to get the Guantanamo prison camp closed, end the indefinite-detention scheme it spawned, and tear down the wall of impunity around officials who ran the torture program there. He is coauthor of several books, most recently *Hell No: Your Right to Dissent in 21st-Century America* (2011) and *Who Killed Che? How the CIA Got Away with Murder* (2011). The *National Law Journal* named him one of the 100 most influential lawyers in the United States.

Ronald Reosti was born in Detroit in 1938. His parents, both from Italy, imparted to him a working-class identity, a sense of social justice, a belief in the possibility of social change, a commitment to democracy, and a hatred of the undemocratic ruling class. He embraced socialism in his early teens, during the McCarthy era, and has remained committed to its principles. For the last forty-eight years he has practiced law and been part of the radical community in Detroit. He looks forward to a vibrant socialist movement to win the millions yearning for an alternative to the inequitable and destructive capitalist system.

Debby Smith has been a socialist since going to college in Boston in the radical sixties provided the atmosphere that encouraged her to question all of society's assumptions. She worked full-time for the anti-Vietnam War movement, the Kent State Legal Defense Fund, and in the feminist, union, and socialist movements. She is a longtime supporter of the Brecht Forum/New York Marxist School. She participates in the anti-capitalist and pro-democracy movements that are growing so rapidly in the United States and worldwide.

Michael Steven Smith is a New York City attorney and author. His most recent book, written with Michael Ratner, is *Who Killed Che? How the CIA Got Away with Murder*. He is on the boards of the Center for Constitutional Rights and the Brecht Forum/New York Marxist School. He was educated at the University of Wisconsin in the 1960s, where he learned social history from the great teacher Harvey Goldberg. He has testified on Palestinian rights before committees of the US Congress and the United Nations. He cohosts the radio show *Law and Disorder* (lawanddisorder.org) on WBAI-FM with Michael Ratner and Heidi Boghosian. He lives with his wife, Debby, and talking parrot, Charlie Parker.

Paul Louis Street is a researcher, writer, and speaker based in Iowa City, Iowa. He is the author of *Empire and Inequality:*

America and the World Since 9/11 (Paradigm, 2004); *Segregated Schools: Educational Apartheid in the Post-Civil Rights Era* (Routledge, 2005); *Racial Oppression in the Global Metropolis: A Living Black Chicago History* (Rowman & Littlefield, 2007); *Barack Obama and the Future of American Politics* (Paradigm, 2008); *The Empire's New Clothes: Barack Obama in the Real World of Power* (Paradigm, 2010); and, with Anthony DiMaggio, *Crashing the Tea Party: Mass Media and the Campaign to Remake American Politics* (Paradigm, 2011).

Steven Wishnia has worked as an editor, reporter, proofreader, substitute teacher, taxi driver, photographer, and musician. He has written and/or edited for numerous national magazines (*High Times, PC, Junior Scholastic*) and leftist publications (Alternet.org, the *Progressive*, the *Nation*, the *Indypendent*, the late *Guardian* newsweekly, and the New York housing monthly *Tenant/Inquilino*). He has won two awards for his reporting on New York housing issues. Bass player and cofounder of the 1980s punk-rock band False Prophets (CD reissue: *Blind Roaches and Fat Vultures*, Alternative Tentacles), he still plays music quasi-professionally. He is the author of *When the Drumming Stops*, a novel (Manic D Press, 2012); *Exit 25 Utopia*, a short-story collection, and *The Cannabis Companion*. His Web site is www.stevenwishnia.com.

Richard D. Wolff, professor emeritus of economics, University of Massachusetts–Amherst, is a visiting professor at New School University in New York. His recent publications include *Occupy the Economy: Challenging Capitalism*, with David Barsamian (2012); *Contending Economic Theories: Neoclassical, Keynesian, and Marxian*, with Stephen Resnick (2012); and *Democracy at Work: A Cure for Capitalism* (2012). He hosts *Economic Update* weekly on WBAI-FM. He writes regularly for the *Guardian* and Truthout.org and has been interviewed on *Democracy Now!, The*

Charlie Rose Show, *Alternative Radio*, and many other programs. The *New York Times Magazine* named him "America's most prominent Marxist economist." His work can be found at rdwolff.com and democracyatwork.info.

Michael Zweig is a professor of economics and director of the Center for the Study of Working-Class Life at Stony Brook University. His most recent books are *The Working Class Majority: America's Best Kept Secret* (Cornell University Press, 2012), and *What's Class Got to Do with It: American Society in the Twenty-first Century* (Cornell University Press, 2004). He was a founding member of Students for a Democratic Society and the Union for Radical Political Economics. He is active in his union, United University Professions (American Federation of Teachers) and has been named "citizen of the year" by *The Suffolk Times* for his writing and community organizing on eastern Long Island.

Index

Wall Street Journal, 11, 189, 241
Walmart, 12, 137, 189, 236, 237
Walton, James "Bud," 12
Walton, Sam, 12, 163
Walton family, 12
wars, 201
  in Iraq, Afghanistan, and Pakistan, 244
  science and, 181–82
Washington Post, 13
weapons, 182
welfare, 127, 130–33
Whirlpool Corporation, 4–5, 9–10
Whitman, Walt, 253
Wisconsin State Life Insurance Fund, 36
Wishnia, Steven:
  biography of, 293
  on drugs, 105–11
W. L. Gore, 35
Wolff, Richard D.:
  biography of, 293–94
  on the shape of a post-capitalist future, 43–51
Woman's Peace Party, 91
women, 89–97, 257
  feminism and, 92–93, 104, 213
  workday of, 85–87
Women's International League for Peace and Freedom (WILPF), 91
work, 5–6, 48–49, 81–84, 104, 127–28

insecurity in, 127–28, 129, 132
minimum wage for, 238
outsourcing of, 6–7, 82–83, 118, 201
paid parental leave from, 82
right to, 73
security in, 78–79
split workweeks, 48–49
time off from, 78, 82, 83
unemployment, 5, 9, 81, 129, 130
wages for, 14, 82–83, 127, 128, 130, 132, 238
woman's workday in a socialist USA, 85–87
worker-owned and -controlled businesses, 34–37, 39, 78–79
workers, corporations and, 44–45
working class, 220, 221, 252–53, 255, 257
World Trade Organization, 143
World War II, 40, 96, 223
Wright, Erik Olin, 36

Yazzie, Robert, 65
Yoo, John, 207

Zetkin, Clara, 94
Zeus, 179
Zweig, Michael:
  biography of, 294
  Occupy Wall Street speech of, 219–22